Margaret Withers taught music in p...
Inner London for 20 years before beco...
for Rochester in 1989. She became i...
support for voluntary children's leaders ... p...
Children's Officer for the Diocese of Chelmsford, she established children's work as an integral part of Reader training as well as providing a similar input to several theological courses. In 2001, she was appointed the Archbishop's Officer for Evangelism among Children, when she spent five years heightening the profile of children and the need to reach a new generation with the gospel message.

Margaret retained her interest in teaching as a chairman of governors, training as an Ofsted inspector, and by promoting the opportunities for churches and schools working together through writing and providing training at theological institutions and as part of CME. She is author of several books published by Barnabas, including the perennially popular Welcome to the Lord's Table and Where are the Children? She is joint author of Creative Communion, which was published by Barnabas in 2008.

Text copyright © Margaret Withers 2010
The author asserts the moral right
to be identified as the author of this work

Published by
The Bible Reading Fellowship
15 The Chambers, Vineyard
Abingdon OX14 3FE
United Kingdom
Tel: +44 (0)1865 319700
Email: enquiries@brf.org.uk
Website: www.brf.org.uk
BRF is a Registered Charity

ISBN 978 1 84101 586 6

First published 2010
10 9 8 7 6 5 4 3 2 1 0
All rights reserved

Acknowledgments
Unless otherwise stated, scripture quotations are taken from the Contemporary English
Version of the Bible published by HarperCollins Publishers, copyright © 1991, 1992, 1995
American Bible Society.

Scripture quotations taken from the Holy Bible, New International Version, copyright © 1973,
1978, 1984, 1995 by International Bible Society. Used by permission of Hodder & Stoughton
Publishers, a member of the Hachette Livre UK Group. All rights reserved. 'NIV' is a registered
traemark of International Bible Society. UK trademark number 1448790.

A catalogue record for this book is available from the British Library

Printed in Singapore by Craft Print International Ltd

Local church, local school

Practical and creative ways for churches to serve local primary schools

Margaret Withers

To David Herbert

Acknowledgments

The subject of this book is very broad and would not have been written without the help of many people who generously gave me their time and expertise. Thank you:

Alison Withers
Ann Mackenzie
Antony Homer
Chris Dench
Chris Hudson
Christopher Smith
Clive Jones
Dawn Watkins
Geoff Brown
Louise Warner
Michael Smith
Paul Cudby
Paul Seaton-Burn
Rona Orme
Stephen Venner

for allowing me to interview you and sending me stories.

Thank you, Jan Thompson and David Herbert, for your specialist contributions on governors, pastoral care, RE and worship; Martyn Payne for contributing the afterword; and all three of you for reading and offering words of wisdom on the final manuscript.

Last but not least, thank you, Sue Doggett for the hours you spent editing the various drafts and for your constant encouragement when I thought it would never be finished!

Contents

Foreword   6

Introduction: the biblical perspective   8

1   Christian vocation   11

2   Christianity and schools   18

3   Schools as part of God's mission   24

4   Forming a relationship with a local school   30

5   Legislation and best practice   38

6   Collective worship in school   51

7   School as a praying community   67

8   The Eucharist in school   75

9   Religious Education, PSHE and Citizenship   86

10 Schools visiting churches   96

11 Clubs and the extended school day   110

12 Voluntary help   124

13 School governors   130

14 Chaplaincy roles in school   139

15 Children's and schools' workers   147

16 Making the school visible to the church   153

17 Churches using school buildings   161

Afterword: Barnabas in schools   170

Appendix 1   Information and websites   174

Appendix 2   Step-by-step through a school Eucharist   177

Appendix 3   Church visit evaluation form   182

Notes   183

Index of subjects   187

*

Foreword

The 19th-century pastor and children's author George MacDonald said that 'It is better to be a child in a green field than a knight of many orders'. This is just what I felt like as I read Margaret Withers' most recent book, *Local Church, Local School*. I was a child again, surrounded by the vast array of options that are available when the Church awakens to the school on its doorstep. There is little doubt that the interface between church and school is the single most strategic engagement for mission, for education or for influence. It is a veritable playground for the theologian, the pastor, the parent, the governor or the lay Christian, as well as the teacher and the child.

This book brings together the developed insights of an author who demonstrates a lifetime of engaged and reflected involvement in children and their environment. As such, the book is timely, being published just before the 200th anniversary of the birth of the Church of England's National Society (and the arrival of free education for all) in 2011. It comes at a time when Christians are pleasantly surprised to be in demand for their interest and involvement in education, and at a point when an authoritative and researched tome is in demand.

To my delight, *Local Church, Local School* is instantly accessible, with accurate practical advice and imaginative theological and reflective ideas. It is a book which must be read by Christian people wanting to be effective in schools, whether professionally or in volunteering mode. I hope it will be on reading lists at theological colleges, training students for contextual ministry. I also see it being kept on the vicarage shelf for specific consultation by the ministry team. It must find its way too into the hands of governors and occasional visitors to school and be the current reference point for diocesan directors of education and school chaplains.

Whatever the readership, I dare to hope that this publication is part of a new groundswell of confidence in the churches. So read it as an encounter with opportunity—namely a dose of vibrancy and enthusiasm, backed up by realism that shows the possibilities God is giving to the Church in the 21st century.

Howard Worsley
Director of Education, Diocese of Southwell and Nottingham

*

— Introduction —

The biblical perspective

These are things we learnt from our ancestors, and we will tell them to the next generation. We won't keep secret the glorious deeds and the mighty miracles of the Lord. God gave his Law to Jacob's descendants, the people of Israel. And he told our ancestors to teach their children, so that each new generation would know his Law and tell it to the next. Then they would trust God and obey his teachings, without forgetting anything God had done.

PSALM 78:3–7

It is evening and the whole family is gathered around the table for dinner. Candles are lit; the best crockery and silver are sparkling; special food has been prepared and served. Toasts are drunk, news is shared and stories are told. You can decide where this meal is taking place. It could be in almost any part of the world and in almost any century.

Suddenly, the youngest child turns to his father. 'Why is tonight different from all the other nights?' he asks. 'On all other nights, we eat either leavened bread or "Matza"; on this night, only Matza.' And, as the Passover moon shines through the window, the father retells the story of how God delivered his ancient people, the Jewish nation, out of slavery in Egypt to freedom in the promised land.

In the Bible we read how Moses commanded the Jewish people to hand down this message of their deliverance to their descendants:

Some day your children will ask, 'Why did the Lord give us these laws and teachings?' Then you will answer: We were slaves of the king of Egypt, but the Lord used his great power and set us free… The Lord rescued us from Egypt, so he could bring us into this land, as he had promised our ancestors. That's why the Lord our God demands that we obey his laws and worship him with fear and trembling. (Deuteronomy 6:20–21, 23–24)

Over the centuries, this has evolved into a ceremonial meal. A significant point is that the youngest child is at the centre of the ceremony. He asks the questions; his father teaches him through his replies and reminds the whole family of the story. The ritual is a response to God's command to hand down the story that gave his people identity at times of persecution and assured them of their role as his chosen people.

Jesus gave children a central place in his teaching. In the prevailing culture, children were ignored in public, but he welcomed them, called them 'signs of his kingdom' and was harsh with the disciples who wanted to marginalise them. As we have noted, children played a central part in Jewish celebrations and the early Jewish church would have continued this practice. Children were part of the household and would have been present when Christians met in homes for teaching, prayers and the breaking of bread.

In Ephesians 6:1, Paul addresses children directly: 'Children, you belong to the Lord, and you do the right thing when you obey your parents.' Then he reminds parents of the way that they should treat their children: 'Parents, don't be hard on your children' (v. 4). The style of his writing indicates that the children would have been present with the rest of their families, listening to his letter being read to them.

How do we continue to tell the story of our salvation to today's children? The Church and children's education have always been closely linked; indeed, they were almost inseparable until the time of the Reformation. Today, a significant number of children are educated in Christian schools, but not every child goes to a church school. Even fewer attend church. Family life is no longer based around shared meals and there is no guarantee that parents will know the Christian story or be willing to tell it.

This book has been written to encourage local churches to see their local school as a place where they can live out their Christian calling to 'tell the story' in today's culture. This can be as much through presence and practical support as through teaching and leading worship, and has the added bonus of giving confidence to schools to see their local church as a teaching resource as well as a community with much to offer.

Christian vocation

'Where your treasure is, there your heart will be also... Seek first [God's] kingdom and his righteousness.'

MATTHEW 6:21, 33 (NIV)

Every day we are faced with hundreds of choices. Some of them involve a selection between two unimportant actions: what to eat for supper or whether to travel by car or on foot. We often make these choices almost mechanically. Other choices are more difficult and take time to think through. They have long-term consequences for ourselves and for the people around us. Behind all these choices, however, lies a fundamental choice about how we live and the direction we follow as individuals. Once that choice is made, the smaller decisions tend to follow automatically. That is why the basic decisions matter so much. If a life has no clear focus, it leads to confused and inconsistent choices with the resulting lack of direction.

The idea of vocation is closely bound up with choice. If choice is an inescapable part of daily life and rests on that fundamental choice of direction, then vocation by implication encompasses the whole of life.

Responding to a call

Perhaps you are wondering why there is a chapter about vocation so early in this book, or even here at all. The very term 'vocation' sounds dramatic and mysterious, and a long way from the playground of a local primary school. The word comes from the Latin *vocare*, which means 'to call' or 'to summon'. It implies that there is someone to do the calling and that the call is asking the listener to move from one state or position to another. It suggests a new way of living or a new task.

In practice, as Christians we believe that God calls each one of us. He invites us to a way of being or to perform some particular task. This means that God has his own plan for every person and that we need to hear and accept his call. It involves responding to him and committing ourselves to his service in whatever position or place he invites us to be.

Like many other religious words, 'vocation' has become part of everyday vocabulary and changed its meaning. It often means little more than a change of job or career. 'Vocational guidance' helps people to sort out what they want from life and how to use their skills and experience to achieve it; 'vocational training' is education geared towards a particular range of jobs, and so on. This changed meaning has, in turn, affected the Church's understanding of vocation, with a loss of the clear sense that it is God who calls. It can become bound up with individual feelings and needs, but we are not unrelated individuals. We are in relationships within our families and our various communities, and we share a common humanity. God calls us into existence, he calls us to be a holy people, and then he brings a particular call to each individual person within that context.

Within the Church, the word 'vocation' is commonly restricted to the religious life, to ordination and a plethora of authorised lay ministries. A great deal of time and expertise is spent on encouraging and training people for these particular ministries, but it has sometimes led to 'professional' clericalism and the concept of two-tier Christian ministry. Typically, this means that little interest or official support is given to the majority of Christians who live out their baptismal calling 'in the world'.

There is only one answer to the question, 'Do I have a vocation?' That is, 'Yes!' Asking that question is part of living out the Christian life and leads to the search to discover how and where God is inviting us to fulfil our particular calling.

Proclaiming the gospel in our daily lives

Nearly all lay people and some clergy live out their Christian calling in the home, in secular employment and through voluntary service. This inevitably entails close cooperation with people who may not share our Christian faith but are committed to the same values or have common interests or skills.

As Christians, we are called first and foremost to be ourselves, to proclaim the gospel by living out our faith where we are, whatever our means of employment, and particularly as parents or carers of the young and vulnerable members of society. Living out the Christian faith in this way proclaims the gospel by example and presence, which is often more effective than an overtly religious approach. It is also vital to the Church in that it provides links and insights into daily life that can be lacking if the Church becomes too centred on its own needs and perceptions.

■ The council and leaders of a large semi-rural church held a study day led by a visiting senior clergyman. When they gathered, the local minister asked each person to say their name and role in the church. 'No,' interrupted the visiting leader, 'I would like you to tell me what you do when you are not at church.' The ensuing discussion brought to light a wide variety of jobs and hobbies—and also revealed that three people present were unemployed but had not made the situation known to the church family. ■

Biblical accounts of people's callings to particular tasks or ways of living are usually dramatic. The callings of Samuel, Isaiah and Paul are described vividly, with visions and the voice of God being clearly seen and heard. They are recorded as single events, with no reference to any previous experiences, influences and opportunities or to the time these people would have taken in seeking advice and holding themselves open to God's will beforehand. Patience

13

is an integral part of vocation. A sense of calling may take years to develop and will rarely arise from a single dramatic experience.

Called to be in school

Some years ago, there was a car sticker that read, 'If you can read this—thank a teacher.' This clever piece of marketing was designed as a reminder of the valuable part that teachers play in shaping children's lives. After parents and the home, school has the largest influence on children, their daily lives and their long-term future.

This book is about the ways in which individual Christians and church communities can seek to live out their Christian vocation by becoming part of the life of a local school, and how the school can have a fruitful relationship with its local churches. From the church perspective, it is a many-faceted relationship. Principally, however, it is a ministry of service which will include a Christian presence and perhaps an overtly Christian input to the curriculum, worship and decision-making process of the school.

Some Christians will be involved with schools in a voluntary capacity. Others will include involvement as part of their specific ministry as clergy, lay ministers and schools' workers. The largest and possibly the most effective group, however, will be people who are living out their Christian lives as employees of the school. The children see them every day. They build up relationships with their class teacher and teaching assistant. They are told off or consoled by staff in the playground. They meet office staff, meals supervisors and technicians regularly, and the work of the caretaker and cleaners has an effect on their well-being and working environment.

Most of the work connected with a school does not appear to be particularly Christian. Some of it is decidedly unglamorous, but all of it will have an effect on literally thousands of young people and their future directions in life. It is estimated that during a working life of 30 years, a primary class teacher or teaching assistant will have played a significant part in the education and development of between 250 and 1000 children and will have taught far more. Non-teaching staff will be in frequent contact with every child in the school, one way or another. Friends chatting on the Internet years after they have left school demonstrate the influence and often profound effect that teachers and other staff have had on them.

The Church of England, which has so much invested in its schools, recognised this when it wrote in its report on Church schools: 'Unless action is taken by the Church to encourage Christians to see teaching as a valued profession, and to show by its actions how it values Christian teachers, the long-term prospect is daunting.'[1]

The same action needs to be taken to encourage Christians with an appropriate interest or skill to consider supporting and serving a school as a way of living out their Christian life and modelling Christian values through their presence.[2] We proclaim Christ by what we are as much as by what we say, and God is glorified in the simplest of tasks. The following story was told by an elderly man about an experience he had in India at the end of World War II:

As a young man, I visited a leper colony and was shown around by one of the nuns who ran it. I saw the ways that the patients were treated for their condition as well as the projects to help them to lead as full lives as was possible. I was very impressed, but asked her if, as they were a religious community, they taught the Christian faith to their patients. The nun looked at me with withering scorn. 'What do you think all this is about?' she asked.

Be patient!

It can take a lot of courage to offer ourselves for a particular task and even more to accept that God may be calling us to be or do something that will be costly in terms of our time, personal freedom and possibly our work. We shouldn't try to work it out on our own. The story of the call of Samuel relates how he went again and again to his mentor, Eli, for guidance as to where his vocation lay. It took time for Eli to recognise that God was calling Samuel to a particular task. Samuel's response to God led to an unwelcome message that he had to deliver to Eli, but was also the beginning of his ministry as a great prophet (1 Samuel 3:1–20).

It is advisable always to seek out someone such as a minister, vicar or spiritual director for guidance, and be prepared for the decision-making to take time. After his conversion experience, Paul went to Ananias and stayed with him and his fellow disciples for some time before starting his ministry (Acts 9:8–19). In the same way, the Christian community today needs to support and guide people in living out their Christian lives. The gentle 'Have you considered...?' may lead to a firm negative reply but it may also be just the spur someone needs to think further or seek advice.

Sometimes a person may see a need, and feel called to make a difference, but may not be the appropriate person or in the right situation to meet that need. This needs sensitive handling. For example, at a vocations day in Essex, two young women attended the session on working with children and youth. When they were asked what they hoped to gain from the session, one of them said, 'God is calling us to bring young people to know the love of Jesus by taking assemblies in the local secondary school'. How do we start?' It transpired that neither woman had any experience of working with young people or had been inside a school since the day they had left. The leader affirmed their desire to bring young people to Christ but suggested that they were trying to do too much, too fast. She advised them to start by helping with the children's and youth work at their church, and see where that would lead them.

Jesus calls us to be salt and yeast—tiny grains that can make a huge difference (Matthew 5:13). He also commands us, 'Make your light shine, so that others will see the good that you do and will praise your Father in heaven' (v. 16). Ways of working this out in the world of education form the substance of the rest of this book.

Christianity and schools

The Church's commitment to the provision of education extends over many centuries. It was most powerfully evident in its drive for the mass provision of Christian education for the poor in the early and middle years of the nineteenth century. Its principal instrument was the National Society, created in 1811. By the time of the national census of 1851, 40 years later, the Church had established 17,000 schools.

THE WAY AHEAD: CHURCH OF ENGLAND SCHOOLS IN THE NEW MILLENNIUM
(ARCHBISHOPS' COUNCIL, 2000)

In 1780, Robert Raikes, a philanthropic journalist and prison visitor, was concerned about the welfare of the children in the Sooty Alley area of Gloucester. Raikes believed that the underlying cause of crime was ignorance, so he started a Sunday school to teach the children to 'read the Bible and keep the Sabbath'. Over the next few years, Sunday schools were set up all over the country. A few taught writing and arithmetic as well as reading. The work grew and the principle of free education for all was soon firmly established. Some Sunday schools became evening classes where adults could gain basic skills. Others eventually became day schools and some of the present-day Church primary schools started in this way.

In 1811, the National Society for the Education of the Poor in the Principles of the Established Church throughout England and Wales was formed.[1] Its aim was to found and maintain a Church school in every parish. In 1814, Joseph Lancaster, a Quaker, founded the British and Foreign Schools' Society to educate poor children through a monitor system. By the end of the 19th century, about 50 per cent of children were educated in schools run by the National Society (known as 'national schools') and other denominational bodies. They became collectively known as 'voluntary schools'. The following story gives a brief picture of such a school in the early 20th century and the beginnings of the development of education for girls from poor families.

Penge lies to the south of the Crystal Palace and the National Sports stadium at the foot of Crystal Palace Hill. In the early 19th century it was a village but, when the canal and the railways were built, immigrants from Ireland and Liverpool moved in to work as labourers. The area was poor and unhealthy. The polluted canal brought typhoid and diphtheria. Several families lived together in tiny cottages, with a pub on every corner (27 in 1880) and a pawnbroker's next door to it. In 1873, the parish church funded a school in a tin 'chapel of ease'.[2] It was 'for the children of the labouring poor'. The school soon grew too big for the chapel so the girls and infants were rehoused in the local market. It charged fees of 3d a week, with 2d for 'those of labouring classes and below'.

From 1899, all children went to school until they were 12. Before 1918, the girls were taught cooking, sewing and laundry so that they could get work in service, but the Great War showed that women should be educated to do other work. This school in Penge was one of the first to give girls a general education that included PE and games lessons in the park and opportunities for exceptionally able girls to sit scholarship exams to the grammar school. Links with the parish church were strong. The vicar took assemblies and gave Religious Instruction to every class. The children sang 'God that madest earth and heaven' at the end of every Friday afternoon.

The school now has a modern building and is an Aided school in the diocese of Rochester. It still maintains its relationship with the local church.

Universal education

The state took responsibility for education in 1870, when the Forster Education Act ordered that schools should be provided for all children. If there were not enough places in the voluntary schools in each district, board schools would be built and paid for by the rates. The aim was to provide schooling for every child. The Religious Education in them was non-denominational and, in some cases, was left to the Sunday schools. Education was not free, except for the poorest children, until 1891.[3]

Attending Sunday school was not the only way that children learned about the Christian faith. The entire state educational system was based on Christian culture and practice. The children of wealthy families were educated at public schools (some originally founded by religious orders during the Middle Ages), where they attended daily worship in chapel and were automatically prepared for confirmation.

Voluntary schools provided a distinctive Christian education. Boys were recruited from them into church choirs. This gave them experience of the Book of Common Prayer, and they were expected to learn and recite the Collect for the week and a biblical text each Sunday. The parish clergy were in the school frequently to lead worship and teach Religious Instruction, often known as 'Scripture' or 'Divinity'.

■ A certificate from the diocese of Chichester was presented to Charlie Verrall for passing his exam in Divinity. It was signed by the curate of Hellingly Church and dated July 1909. Charlie was aged 6. ■

In 1918, the school leaving age was raised to 14. Most children stayed at the same elementary school throughout their school lives, with the most able children moving to fee-paying grammar schools at the age of 11.

Primary schools and the effect on Christian education

In 1944, the Butler Education Act made radical changes to state education. Religious Education (RE) and a daily act of worship became compulsory unless children were withdrawn by their parents. The school leaving age was raised to 15 years. The elementary schools became primary schools, and every child moved to a secondary school at 11. Many new secondary schools had no formal links with the Church, so many young people thought of religion as something 'childish'.

Social changes, including the post-war break-up of communities, development of urban housing estates and the popularity of television in the early 1950s, destroyed many families' links with their relatives and familiar communities—including the local church. For many children, the only place where they learned anything about Christianity was in school or through youth activities. Daily Christian assembly and RE were part of every child's education and many children belonged to uniformed organisations, choirs and other church-based groups. Until the mid-1960s, most adults could say the Lord's Prayer and sing a few Christmas carols and well-known hymns at weddings and funerals.

Rising secularism

This was not to last. Society was becoming secularised and the Christian principles that underpinned the educational system were being questioned. Practising a religion was considered to be a personal matter. Worship and teaching about the Christian faith in school and children's organisations was discouraged, even in some Church schools, and quality was often poor. The place of RE in state schools was frequently discussed and even questioned.

In 1970, the Church of England's report *The Fourth R*[4] stated that the role of RE in Church schools was educational, not evangelistic, and had different aims from the teaching provided by the local church. RE became, increasingly, the provision of information about different religions and ignored the need for children to learn about religious experience and practices. Some RE teachers were so anxious to be objective that they discouraged children from mentioning their personal faith or anything they had experienced in church. Schools and uniformed organisations severed their contact with their local churches and, by the 1970s, even traditional events like carol concerts and nativity plays were often marginalised. These developments dechurched the nation: many children were brought up with little or no knowledge of the Christian faith, and those children are today's parents.

The present situation

The late 1980s and early 1990s were a time of major change for children, with far-reaching legislation about their care and education. The Children Act (1989) changed thinking about the rights of the child as well as improving standards of care. The 1988 Education Reform Act established the National Curriculum alongside RE. It transformed the teaching of RE and acts of worship. The spiritual life of the school and its worship had to be assessed as part of regular Ofsted[5] inspections.

The Education Reform Act (1988) also allowed schools to opt out of local authority control and become grant-maintained.[6] Many grant-maintained Church schools became more consciously Christian as they strengthened their links with their local churches and diocesan Boards of Education. Standards improved through having denominational inspections of worship and RE.[7]

Today, for a variety of reasons, there is a more positive attitude to religion in school, although there are frequent attempts to curtail the influence of faith schools on the grounds that they are elitist or divisive. This situation offers both challenges and opportunities to churches in forming relationships with schools and is discussed in the next two chapters.

＊

— 3 —

Schools as part of God's mission

You serve first. Jesus did not say, 'I will only love you when you have followed me.'

PAUL WAKELIN, VICAR OF ALL SAINTS' PERRY STREET, GRAVESEND, 1996–2006,
DISCUSSING MISSION

What is a school?

The word 'school' usually calls to mind several distinctive images. We may think of children in uniform clustered around low tables or sitting in a circle on the floor, or possibly streaming out of the school gate at the end of the afternoon. Another image is of a building designed for children, with an open space for play and perhaps a sports field.

But a school is far more than a building. It is a community created to enable children to learn and to be taught. It contains people of all ages and backgrounds: pupils, teachers, teaching assistants, non-teaching staff, parents, governors and members of the local community. Some urban primary schools may have up to 30 languages spoken, with members of differing economic and social backgrounds, from different faiths and cultures. Others will have fewer than 100 pupils and be at the centre of a small rural community.

Many people think of schools as being no-go areas, surrounded with security fences and locked gates, demanding endless paper-work before a visitor can step through the door. Although security is often high and can appear daunting, most schools are friendly and welcoming communities that appreciate interest and support from the local community, including churches and other faith communities.

The spiritual dimension of education

In Chapter 2 we saw how, after the Industrial Revolution, the Church became a pioneer in providing free education for all, especially in deprived areas. It can be justly proud of this, but, with the changes in post-war society and its rapid secularisation, the number of children who have an opportunity to hear the Christian story has been devastated over the last 50 years. Today, we have two and possibly three generations of people who know little, if anything, about the Christian faith.

But there are signs of hope. It is widely accepted that humans are spiritual creatures and embark on a spiritual journey from birth. Educationalists and sociologists are beginning to recognise the damage that has been done by trivialising religious belief and secularising our culture. It is acknowledged that there is more to education than learning facts, and that neglecting the spiritual development of the child hinders his or her growth as a whole person. Spiritual development forms part of Ofsted inspections, alongside social, moral and cultural development. Religious Education and 'broadly Christian' acts of worship are integral parts of the curriculum and only a few parents refuse permission for their children to attend religious services or visit places of worship. Increasing numbers of clergy are leading worship in school or inviting schools to have a service in church at Christmas.

Relationships between schools and churches are being restored as schools now look to the local church for advice on the spiritual dimension of education. Attainment Target 2 in RE is about learning from religion and relating it to one's own experience.[1]

The church perspective

Before his ascension, Jesus commanded his followers, 'You will be my witnesses in Jerusalem, and in all Judea and Samaria, and to the ends of the earth' (Acts 1:8, NIV). Responding to his command is a vital part of living out our Christian lives and should be part of every church's ministry in the community.

England is divided into parishes, many of them dating from medieval times, so every school is set within an Anglican parish. This is an enormous privilege, which is not always appreciated. As every child attends school from the term before his or her fifth birthday, and most communities include children of school age, it is sensible for every church, of whatever denomination, to give high priority to forging relationships with the local school.

Meeting people where they are

The aims of churches working alongside schools include both support and service. Christians want other people to have an opportunity to hear the Christian story and consequently to draw closer to God. This is not a recipe for forcing the Christian faith or personal religious opinions down other people's throats, but it involves being true to the gospel through the way that we live it out. It is about engagement and building relationships. It is about serving each other in the wider community, which includes being prepared to listen to and support people in times of need.

- In a mining village in West Yorkshire, the school is next door to the church and has strong links with it. In the early 1990s, the local pits had closed and the community was at a very low ebb, with a lot of real poverty. In response to this situation, the church ran an all-day holiday club for a week, which included a day at the seaside. This gave children the only holiday they could have, and helped families by providing child care that included meals.

Many clergy and lay people who take on chaplaincy roles firmly believe that the best relationships are built slowly by being present in the staff room, by offering a listening ear at times of celebration as well as sorrow, and by literally crawling around the room with the nursery class or coaching football with Year 6. Leading worship and teaching RE require considerable time and skill and will not necessarily be the first or the best steps, if taken in isolation. Some schools may welcome such help immediately, but in others it will take years to build enough confidence and trust to serve in this way.[2]

Nearly all of Jesus' teaching took place in the street, in the countryside or beside Lake Galilee. He engaged in dialogue with a Samaritan woman with a dubious reputation and had supper with a dishonest tax collector. As with Jesus' own ministry, some of a church's relationship with a school will also be outside the boundaries of Sunday worship and the school day.

■ The parents and children at a primary school in Essex know about the church through its children's programme. About 130 children attend Tumble Tots or Pre-school, where they enjoy different activities as well as having a circle time for worship and sharing news. The children eventually move on to the school, but some of them continue the link by attending the after-school club on Friday or the holiday club during February half-term. The holiday club ends with a disco and prayers on Saturday evening, followed by a thanksgiving service in church on Sunday. ■

Church without walls

A few churches either worship in another church building or use a school or community centre. Some are independent churches; others are distinctive ethnic communities. New developments around major cities often have no church building at all. The church in such places is literally the people of God on the move. They meet in houses, respond to people as opportunities present themselves, and hire a room or hall for a Sunday service. One of their challenges is to provide opportunities for young people and families to meet for activities beyond Sunday morning.[3]

A church in a new development in the East Midlands worships at the community centre on Sunday and at the school on Tuesday, when the curate leads collective worship. In order to reach whole families and offer some simple Christian teaching, he and his wife held an Advent 'Messy Church' in December 2007.[4] It was so successful that they followed it with a similar Easter event. The third event was a Messy Christingle. About 60 children and their parents packed into the school hall to take part in seasonal activities, including making their own Christingles. Many of the activity leaders were on the edge of the church but experiencing Christianity in a practical way.

The afternoon ended with a short Christingle service. For a few seconds, the only light came from the Christingles in children's hands, lighting up their faces as they worshipped Jesus, the light for the world.[5] The silence was a prayer in itself.

Approaching a school

Here are some basic pointers to help you if you are considering making a first approach to a school with a view to building a relationship. Before making your approach, pray for the school during the main Sunday service at the beginning of term, on Education Sunday, during public exams and at any time of need, such as the death of a child or the appointment of a new head teacher. Send a card to the school so that members of the staff know you are aware of a particular situation and are praying about it. When discussing anything to do with working in the wider community or about the church's own children's or youth work, always include the school in the discussion.

Think about people who are already known at the school. Children in the congregation may go there. Adults may work there, be governors or voluntary helpers, or know children who attend the school. Review the church's resources. At the same time as looking at what the church has to offer, find out something about the school's own needs and resources.

Making the first steps towards developing a relationship with your school forms the substance of the next chapter.

✳

— 4 —

Forming a relationship with a local school

Our servant attitude—of putting the schools' educational needs at the heart of everything we do—has been critical to building and sustaining our successful relationship with schools. So has been the way that our lessons enable children to meet and talk to 'real' Christians (people who go to a local church) and to visit those churches too. This helps enliven the sessions and satisfies educational goals. But there is arguably greater value for encouraging churches to reach out to their communities, share their faith more actively and discover that it need not be scary and it's certainly not rocket science!

PAUL HAYNES, RE INSPIRED PROJECT DIRECTOR

Christians in Britain have always been active in education. The first schools were in monastic houses and, as we have read in Chapter 2, the Church was at the forefront of providing free schools for everyone and still has an influence on education at all levels. All state schools must provide RE and daily collective worship. RE is a statutory subject taught to all ages from Reception upwards and reflects the faith communities in Britain by being mostly Christian but including other religions. Collective worship in community schools has to be 'wholly or mainly of a broadly Christian character' but there are wide variations in practice. In Church schools, the worship will be Christian and will follow the practices of the particular denomination. Teachers who are not practising Christians may struggle with leading acts of worship of any kind, so the school may welcome help in these and other areas.

Schools are designed for education. If the local church can

show that its contribution will help to raise standards and provide help to hard-pressed teachers, and that its representatives will respect the school's ethos and regulations, it will be made very welcome.

The first step is to talk through possibilities with the vicar or minister, to seek his or her guidance. Then identify people in the congregation who share an enthusiasm for forming links with a school—perhaps a group of friends, a former teacher, or someone who has been waiting some time for a like-minded person to make the first move.

Next, think about what the church can offer and how the church and school might work together to address some of the needs of children living in the locality. Be clear and honest about the church's aims and the limits of its resources. The church must not go into a school overtly to proselytise but to offer practical help—which, in itself, models Christian values. This will happen only by building a relationship of trust and mutual respect, and that takes time and patience. The church's presence may bear fruit, but the time and way is in the hands of the Lord of the harvest.

A church usually approaches a school by offering help with activities such as leading collective worship or helping with RE. These activities require a great deal of skill and time, so churches with a small congregation, sharing a vicar or minister, may feel that they have little or nothing to offer. There are, however, many other ways in which people can be of service and support a school. They may not be overtly Christian but can actually be the best starting point for a contact.

Think about the church's resources, both in terms of building and the people.[1] Note what the church could offer. Be realistic: some excellent plans fail because the people don't have the time or resources to sustain them. Whatever the church does will have a long-term effect, for good or ill.

Find out a little about the school. Some of the answers to the following questions will be on its website or the Local Authority's.

Others can be answered by chatting to people who are parents or who work at the school.

- What is the age range and number of children?
- How is the school governed?
- Do all the children live locally or do a substantial number travel to school?
- Does the school have any particular interests or specialities?
- What does the most recent Ofsted report say about the school?
- How does the school deliver Religious Education and collective worship?
- What kinds of voluntary help does the school already receive?

If the school is Church Aided or Controlled, it will be a Christian school, with the local clergy and representatives of the church on its governing body. Nearly all such schools are Church of England or Roman Catholic, but there are a few Methodist schools and a tiny number run by smaller denominations. It would be courteous and sensible to contact the relevant clergy first to find if voluntary help would be welcomed.

If there are already Christian groups working in any school, see if your church can be of help elsewhere. If you are considering providing a breakfast or after-school club, find out what is already going on in the area before setting one up.[2]

Warnings

Your clergy and church council should be kept fully informed of any plans to be involved in a school. They are legally responsible for anything that goes on in the name of the church and a vision for schools can become part of the church's mission strategy in the community. Moreover, the permission and prayerful support of the clergy and council will be needed before taking any action.

Schools will take as much time as the church can offer, so don't, in a wave of enthusiasm, take on more than people can easily manage. Schools are very tiring places and the staff will expect helpers to be reliable and punctual. This is a good reason for working as a group, because then people can cover for each other as well as providing mutual support.

Schools are very security-conscious. Helpers will almost certainly be expected to sign the visitors' book and wear a badge when visiting the school. Anybody who goes into school regularly will need an enhanced disclosure certificate from the Criminal Records Bureau.[3] This will be organised by the local authority or, in the case of Church schools, by the denominational officer. All helpers need to understand this requirement. If someone has worshipped at the church for less than five years, it would be advisable to ask for and take up references, including one from their previous church, before allowing them to work with young people in any situation.

Making first contact

Head teachers carry a massive responsibility for leading their staff in delivering their utmost for the children. Some head teachers are better at delegating than others but they are ultimately responsible for the daily running of the school. Something as potentially fruitful as a church–school relationship will need to be approached carefully, once all its implications have been thought through. When meeting with a head teacher for the first time, it is important to be where the school is, in every sense, and to be willing to listen as well as talk.

Members of a church arranged to see the head teacher of the local school. They started by telling her of the things that they could offer to help the school. The Head listened and then said, 'Oh, you are offering to help us. I had assumed that you had come to ask me how we could help you!'

Your church may already have a link within the school through a member of the teaching staff. If not, make an appointment to see the head teacher through the school secretary. Heads are notoriously busy, so give some indication of the reason for seeking a meeting and the length of time needed. At the first meeting it is helpful to introduce yourself and your church, to explain any particular roles—such as that of the minister, children's leader and so on— and to outline how the church would like to offer practical support to the school. Find out if there are ways in which the church could help, and carefully consider any suggestions that are made to you, even if they are not what you had in mind. Talk about what the church has to offer—including the service of individuals as well as the use of buildings. Be careful, though, not to make commitments on behalf of other people: just offer to discuss any suggestions with them.

Follow your visit with a letter or email concerning the discussions, so that everyone is clear about what decisions were made and what further action will be taken. This first contact is important, and so is the church's response to any suggestions from the head teacher. He or she will probably suggest a small or single task, which will almost certainly not involve direct contact with the children. Ask to be introduced to the relevant members of staff, listen to their advice and be prepared to ask questions. If the initial contact goes well, the church will be offered more. Once the school finds that helpers from the church are reliable, capable and genuinely committed, it will be open to other ways in which they can be of assistance.

A history of good relationships between a school and a church can lead to people being invited to take on more significant roles. Schools gain from local church links by acquiring committed helpers whose interest and expertise support the school both inside and outside the classroom. People from outside the school bring new perspectives on the subject in hand. In addition, the service that Christians offer to a school is key in itself. Washing paint pots or making a cup of tea for an exhausted teacher may not seem specifically Christian, but these are practical ways of living out Christian values by serving the local school. Christian service needs to be grounded regularly in prayer, through a prayer group, at Sunday services and as part of personal prayer.

There are many ways for Christians to serve that are not directly faith-based but can benefit the whole school community. Schools will only allow people to work directly with children if they know them to be suitable, and it takes time to build up good relationships.

Timescales

Be realistic when attempting to start a completely new relationship with a school. It will take at least three months to build up a successful picture of both your church's strengths and the needs of the local school, and at least a term to establish any regular task, such as helping in the office on Thursdays or leading a class act of worship once a month. After that, you can start to look at ways in which the church can be of further service. Any help that involves the curriculum, such as a school visit to the church, or providing help with football coaching, will need to be made at least a term in advance. It will be necessary to look at the school calendar to find out when help will be most welcomed, but Christmas and the end of the school year are obvious times.

■ One church offered the local primary school the use of the church building for its Christmas performances. The whole school was involved in the presentation, which involved a traditional nativity, and the vicar was able to add a short meditation and prayer at the end. This led into a further invitation to hold a regular carol concert in the church in which children led the prayers and readings and one of the teachers gave a talk. ■

Keeping the church informed

Let the church know what's happening. Send a report to the church council and write about anything especially interesting in the church magazine. Always indicate intended plans for the near future, as this may encourage other people to help.

Education Sunday is a good day to focus on the church's relationship with the local school. Include the school in the prayers and, if there is time, ask the school if it would be possible for you to create a display of project work in the church.[4]

Sponsorship

Sometimes it may be possible for the church to offer ongoing or one-off sponsorship to its local schools, with donations being made for a specific event or outlay. Sponsorship may be for peripatetic learning, equipment or single events, such as RE days.[5]

Following a fruitful conversation several months ago, a benefactor made a donation to the school to purchase percussion instruments, in order that a Year 6 percussion group could be formed. This allowed us to develop a long-standing interest in drumming, percussion and mime. After a few months' lessons and practice, with a weekly 30-minute lunch-time session, the group reached a level at which they were able to lead worship at school and a church Communion service. They also played at a PTA summer fête, a garden party and their own leavers' service.

Half of that year's drumming group is now involved in the monthly 'Rhythm of God' worship-through-percussion service at the church. This group has also built up dialogue between the children and myself, which has made church seem far more accessible for some of them, which we hope will lead to their own spiritual growth in the coming years. ▉

THE REVD PAUL CUDBY, TANWORTH-IN-ARDEN C OF E PRIMARY SCHOOL

A final thought

When your church has established a relationship with its local schools, it may be possible for you to provide support with the school's RE programme or worship.[6] Clergy or lay leaders who are good communicators or trained teachers can contribute enormously by helping with RE lessons or using their talents and interests in other subjects. If RE is not well funded at the school, the church could offer to donate books for the department or library or sponsor a Barnabas RE Day or similar event.[7] The church could also be associated with the school's particular charity or its link-school in another country.

Legislation and best practice

I've got so many CRB certificates, I could paper my office wall with the things...

GRAHAM NUNN, BARNABAS CHILDREN'S MINISTRY TEAM

Schools are friendly places that welcome visitors, but, like any other community or place of work, they have rules for the safety and well-being of their members and visitors. Some of these rules are the law of the land; others are policies and rules decided by the local education authority or the school governors. Some are guidelines or examples of best practice that help the school to run smoothly and ensure that the staff and children enjoy teaching and learning together in a safe environment. There are also 'common sense' rules, which usually involve being thoughtful and courteous and considering the effects of a decision before acting upon it.

What legislation is there?

Legislation mainly covers child protection and health and safety, but recent legislation supporting the initiative 'Every Child Matters' aims to improve the quality of life for every child. Most legislation is clearly designed for the benefit of all concerned. Unfortunately, the media make the most of the occasional story of extremism, using it to criticise either the legislators or the community concerned. So if your church is considering being involved in a local school, set aside all the stories you've heard and find out what the relevant legislation is and how it is applied in your locality or in the school.

The information needed depends on whether people are going to be in direct contact with children, such as helping with lessons, outings or acts of worship, or assisting in other ways—for example, as a governor or in the school office. Whichever way people are involved, the best place for information is in the school itself. Asking, 'Is there anything we need to know?' will usually result in sensible advice and maybe a checksheet. The local education or diocesan office will also be able to help. For more detailed information, the Office for Standards in Education (Ofsted), the local authority (LA), and the Department for Children, Schools and Families (DCSF) will have lots of information available, including the relevant legislation, on their websites[1] or in the public library. Be warned, however, that most Acts of Parliament are the size of a telephone directory. It's possible to spend many hours ploughing through pages of data just to find a couple of paragraphs or a few lines. It is usually better to ask for advice, see if a factsheet is available, or find help in a book.

Visiting the school in any capacity

If anyone plans to visit the school for any reason, best practice is always to contact the office to find out the best time to do so. The school office is usually in the reception area and no one should attempt to enter the school by any other route. Visitors will be expected to sign the visitors' book and wear a badge. This will not only identify the visitor, preventing him or her from being challenged, but is also for the visitor's own safety, providing a record that he or she is in the building in case of a fire or another emergency. If visitors are attending a lesson, assembly or event, they will be escorted or directed to the correct room, hall or sports field. It is not good practice to wander around the school, however attractive or interesting it may be. It can be disruptive and causes embarrassment to staff who do not know the person or why he or she is there. It is also discourteous: visitors are guests in someone else's place of work and need to respect it.

Anyone who is going to be helping in the school regularly will be expected to undergo a Criminal Records Bureau (CRB) enhanced disclosure. This may not be required for a single visit when individuals are not alone with the children, such as giving a talk or being an extra pair of hands on a class outing.

Legislation concerning children's welfare

The Children Act (1989) was the most far-reaching piece of legislation concerning the welfare of children for over 100 years. It covered every aspect of child care and made the child's welfare paramount. An important aspect addressed by the Act was inappropriate care of children in both the statutory and the voluntary sectors—ranging from safety issues to serious neglect and physical and sexual abuse. One response was to set up a system whereby the police could check whether any individual had a criminal conviction that should preclude them from working with children. This check became mandatory for workers in schools, children's homes and similar institutions, and then in the voluntary sector.

Twenty years on, each major Christian denomination has a child protection policy, which every church is expected to follow. Rather than dealing a death blow to children's and youth work, as had been feared, it has raised the profile of children's work as well as the standards of care. Church councils have been obliged to accept their legal responsibility for all that goes on in the name of the church, and the vast majority have taken their responsibilities seriously. One of those responsibilities is to ensure that anyone who is in unsupervised contact with children has undergone an enhanced disclosure with the Criminal Records Bureau (CRB).

The Criminal Records Bureau

The Criminal Records Bureau (administered by the DCSF) aims to help organisations in the public, private and voluntary sectors by identifying candidates who may be unsuitable to work with children or other vulnerable members of society.

A CRB enhanced disclosure involves checking the applicant's personal details for criminal convictions and other information that may bar them from working with children. The procedure requires the provision of basic information with supporting documentation such as a driving licence, birth certificate, marriage certificate and passport. These are checked against three lists for criminal convictions and other adverse information.

Most denominations or other voluntary organisations have procedures for making the application on the church's behalf. It takes six to eight weeks for the disclosure to be processed and the fee is usually paid by the organisation. For reasons of security, CRB disclosures are not usually transferrable at present, so, if anyone is considering helping in a school, the head teacher will probably ask them to undertake a separate disclosure before working there. This will usually be organised by the local authority. Teachers and other workers in schools are required to reapply every three years.

In January 2009, the new Independent Safeguarding Authority (ISA) took over responsibility for making the decision to bar unsuitable new referrals from working with children. It was created in 2008 as a response to one of the recommendations of the 2004 Bichard Inquiry into the murders of Holly Wells and Jessica Chapman in Soham in 2002. Its purpose was described as 'to help avoid harm, or risk of harm, to children and vulnerable adults. It will aim to do this by preventing those who are deemed unsuitable to work with children and/or vulnerable adults from gaining access to them through their work.'

The ISA carries out its objectives by:

- Working in partnership with the Criminal Records Bureau (CRB), which will gather information on a person who will or wishes to work in regulated or controlled activity with vulnerable groups.
- Using this information to decide on a case-by-case basis if an individual poses a risk of harm to vulnerable groups.
- Securely storing information about people's ISA status for employers and voluntary organisations to use when they are recruiting.

'OUT OF THE OLD AND INTO THE NEW FOR STAFF PROTECTING THE VULNERABLE'
(ISA, 8 SEPTEMBER 2008)

In October 2009, the ISA started to replace the previous scheme. Searches now include police cautions and similar information as well as convictions. In order to encourage high standards of care and to support the valuable service provided by the voluntary sector, registration for volunteers is currently free of charge.[2]

Every Child Matters: change for children

Following the earlier legislation on child protection, the Children Act 2004 has provided the legislative underpinning of a strategy for improving the quality of children's lives: 'Every Child Matters'. The government's aim is for every child, whatever their background or circumstances, to have the support they need to:

- Be healthy
- Stay safe
- Enjoy and achieve
- Make a positive contribution
- Achieve economic well-being

Described as 'a shared national programme of change', it aims to encourage organisations that provide services to children—

including hospitals, schools, police and voluntary groups—to work together in order to protect children and young people from harm and help them to achieve the best things in life. The declared ambition is 'to improve those outcomes for all children and to narrow the gap in outcomes between those who do well and those who do not'.

Working with children in school

There is a variety of ways for people to be of service to a school by helping with lessons and other activities.[3]

Best practice

Each child and adult is of intrinsic value and made in the image of God. This may be difficult to remember at times, but the children who have learning or behavioural difficulties, or the teacher who is being hostile, are in need of extra caring, not less. Helpers should always speak to children as they would expect to be spoken to themselves. Personal and insulting language, such as, 'Don't be stupid,' should be avoided, as should the use of physical contact to deal with unsatisfactory behaviour. Disciplinary issues should always be referred to the teacher. The aim is to be of service to the school community, whether it is by making coffee, hearing children read or helping with particular lessons. The school's rules and procedures should always be supported, even if we do not personally agree with them.

Visitors are certain to meet children whom they know outside school. Anyone visiting or working in a school must guard against singling out children because they know them and should never stop to speak to an individual child in the middle of a lesson or when the children are walking from one room to another. If a child waves at a visitor, the visitor should just smile to acknowledge it. Most children know the boundaries and will behave accordingly. It is also important to be discreet. Helpers will learn a lot about children and their families, including information about their personal lives and educational and medical needs. Such information should never be discussed outside school. If a helper feels that a particular piece of outside knowledge would be useful, he or she should seek advice from someone in authority, such as the class teacher—for example, 'Sarah burst into tears when she was asked to read in Sunday school. May I explain to the leader that she is dyslexic?' Children should never be invited to a helper's home, offered lifts in a car or visited out of school hours.

While, as Christians, we long for the people we meet to come to know the love of God, we must not seek to convert pupils or invite them to church. That is an abuse of the school's hospitality. This does not mean, however, that Christianity is a no-go area.

Legislation: The National Curriculum, RE and worship

The National Curriculum is a framework used by all maintained schools to ensure that teaching and learning are balanced and consistent. It has led to enormous changes in the way that children are taught and expected to learn. Following the independent investigation and report, *Thinking Primary*,[4] radical changes to make the primary curriculum more flexible are under discussion and should be fully operational by 2011. In this respect, many helpers will find that the school they visit is very different from their own school or even that of their children.

The National Curriculum sets out the subjects taught, along with the knowledge, skills and understanding required. Each subject has standards or attainment targets so that teachers can measure the child's progress and plan the next steps in their learning.

Each school is regularly inspected by Ofsted. The school's latest inspection report will be found on the Ofsted website or in the local public library. The school may be able to lend a summary of the report, which would probably be sufficient for a church's needs.

Many teachers and children have responded well to working within this framework, but there is currently some concern that creative subjects such as music and drama are being squeezed out and that lack of time and space to play may be a factor in some of the increased behavioural difficulties in very young children. On the other hand, although many schools use the Qualifications and Curriculum Development Agency (QCDA), which has replaced the Qualifications and Curriculum Authority (QCA) schemes of work, to plan their lessons, they are free to organise their teaching in the way that best meets the needs of their children, so a creative plan of work may address these concerns.

The National Curriculum is organised into blocks of years called 'Key Stages' (KS). There are four Key Stages as well as an 'Early Years Foundation Stage', which covers education for children before they reach five, the compulsory school starting age.

The following table shows how old you should expect the children to be, when working in a particular class or year group.

Age in years	Stage	Year group
3–4	Early Years Foundation Stage	(Pre-school or nursery)
4–5	Early Years Foundation Stage	Reception
5–6	KS 1	Year 1
6–7	KS 1	Year 2
7–8	KS 2	Year 3
8–9	KS 2	Year 4
9–10	KS 2	Year 5
10–11	KS 2	Year 6

Currently, there are Standard Assessment Tasks (SATs) in English and Mathematics in the summer term of Year 2 and in the summer term of Year 6 in England. There are no tests in Wales or Scotland and there is mounting pressure to remove some of the SATs from primary schools in England.

Religious Education is compulsory but is organised differently from the rest of the National Curriculum. Each local authority has a Standing Advisory Council for Religious Education (SACRE), which decides the local RE curriculum to be followed in all foundation and Church Controlled schools. (Church Aided schools have their own curriculum.)[5]

Worship

Each school has a compulsory daily act of worship, which is still often called 'assembly'. It is conducted in a variety of ways, from a gathering of the whole school to smaller meetings in year groups or classes, but all assemblies have to be recorded and will form part of an inspection. In community schools, worship is described as 'broadly Christian'. This implies not a benign neglect of any religious input but an acceptance that every school will be composed of children and adults of all faiths and none. Topics will include Bible stories and may look at subjects that are of interest from the perspective of different religions and cultures.

Faith schools will have acts of worship according to their religious denomination. Many Christian schools are communities in which the life of the school is based on prayer, and Christian faith is not only taught but also lived out.

The legislation about worship in school is complex. Anyone who hopes to be involved with a school's worship will need to know what is required and what they may not do. The school concerned will be able to provide the church with the information needed, especially if they have an accurate and up-to-date policy statement on collective worship in their school.[6]

Legislation: Learning outside the classroom

In November 2006, the government launched its *Learning Outside the Classroom* manifesto. It set out a plan to redress the balance between formal lessons in the classroom and the use of the world beyond as an integral part of children's education and personal development. Its stated vision is, 'We believe that every young person should experience the world beyond the classroom as an essential part of learning and personal development, whatever their age, ability or circumstances.'[7] (*Learning Outside the Classroom*, p. ii)

The manifesto, which is attractive and well worth reading, encourages teachers to use visits and facilities to promote learning and improve educational standards by enabling children to learn through experience. These will include visits to places such as museums and art galleries as well as local open spaces and countryside. One effect of this legislation is that schools are actively exploring ways of using the local environment to support and enhance the curriculum. This gives churches a wonderful opportunity to be involved, providing people who can help with class visits and outside activities. The church and the grounds are also excellent resources in themselves.[8]

Going on visits

Class visits can be some of the most rewarding teaching experiences, but take a lot of organisation and planning. Parents and other helpers are always needed to escort the children and help them with their work, so individuals who know the children, perhaps from helping occasionally in class, are always welcome. Helpers should be prepared to work hard and end up exhausted! The children will be excited. They will be in a strange setting, perhaps travelling on public transport. Helpers will probably be given a group to supervise and will need to be firm, encouraging the children to remain calm and sensible. It is important to support the staff by doing exactly as they request, making sure that the group is back at the meeting place on time and never taking children away from the area where they are working. During school trips, teachers will often divide the class into small groups of four to five children, each accompanied by an adult. If a helper is in charge of a group, he or she needs to ensure that it is always within sight or hearing of another group.

At meal breaks, sweets or other food should not be offered to the children. Such practice singles out individual children and could be dangerous if a child suffers from a particular allergy. If a child has forgotten his or her lunch or has an inadequate lunch, helpers should speak to the teacher in charge of the class.

Criteria for governance of schools

The criteria for the governance of different schools and their religious practice fall under three headings. The chart opposite describes Church of England schools, but the criteria would apply to any faith schools.

The legal responsibilities of being a school governor can seem daunting but local authorities, dioceses and schools always welcome and value governors. New governors are supplied with handbooks and training to support their work.[9]

School	Church Aided	Church Controlled	Community
Governing body	Church (foundation) governors have an absolute majority of places. The parish priest is usually an ex officio member.	Church (foundation) governors have a minority of places. The parish priest is usually an ex officio member.	No formal church representation among governors.
Collective worship	Reflects the Anglican tradition and can include worship in the parish church.	Reflects the Anglican tradition and can include worship in the parish church.	Majority of acts of worship should be of a broadly Christian character.
RE curriculum	Governors determine a syllabus that reflects the Anglican tradition. They may make use of a diocesan syllabus where it exists.	Local agreed syllabus unless the parents request a denominational one. The foundation governors have rights of appointment of 'reserved teachers' to teach denominational RE.	Local agreed syllabus.
Church services	Parental right of withdrawal from attendance at services.	Parental right of withdrawal from attendance at services.	Parental permission required for a child to attend a service in church.
Inspection	Ofsted inspectors look at most issues. Denominational inspectors inspect RE, worship and school ethos.	Ofsted inspectors look at general issues and RE. Denominational inspectors look at RE and may report on school ethos.	Ofsted inspectors conduct the whole inspection.

A final thought

Some people are reluctant to help in schools because they are intimidated by the legislation and rules. These need not be a cause for concern. If the school policies and the example of experienced members of the teaching staff are followed, the legalities should look after themselves. The important thing is to listen and learn and, if you are not sure, just ask!

6

Collective worship in school

A young team vicar in Yorkshire had one secondary and four primary schools in his parish. He visited each of them every week and often took an assembly. One day he complained to a senior colleague that his work in the schools took up too much time. His colleague listened carefully, then said, 'Tell me, what is it like to have a congregation of over 2000 every week?'

Everyone who reads this book will have attended an act of worship in school at some time. Some will remember when it was called 'prayers' and included a hymn, a Bible reading and the Lord's Prayer. More people will have experienced 'assembly', which was sometimes a creative presentation by a class on a topical subject, or involved listening to a story with an underlying moral message. Those whose experience was in a Church school, however, may have attended Christian worship that was the centre of the life of the community.[1] Worship has been part of daily life in almost every school in Britain for centuries and has been compulsory since the Butler Education Act in 1944.

One of the legacies of that Act is that it set down the roots of spiritual development as part of the education of the whole child. At that time, spirituality was seen to be identical with Christian worship, but, with research into spiritual development carried out during the past 30 years, it has come into its own as encapsulating the qualities that make us human.

Changes in school worship in the last 75 years

Since 1944, Britain has become a more secular society, yet with a more diverse religious and cultural identity. As the culture has changed, schools have responded differently to their obligation to provide worship, given that many staff have felt unwilling to impose a particular faith on children from such diverse backgrounds, especially when they did not honestly believe in it themselves. By 1970, some assemblies consisted of a song and a story on a moral theme, followed by time for reflection. A few schools had separate assemblies for staff and pupils of different faiths. Others delivered worship that was Christian in subject but designed to be acceptable to those of all faiths and none.

■ In 1979, an inner-city primary school with a strong multi-ethnic mix of children decided that it was inappropriate to continue to say the Lord's Prayer at every assembly. The staff still felt, however, that they needed some sort of special prayer that everyone could join in. They decided to sing the prayer of St Francis, 'Make me a channel of your peace', as it reflected the community's common values and transcended different religious practices. ■

The Education Reform Act of 1988 attempted to address the situation with a complicated statement on the character and place of worship in school:

All pupils in attendance at a maintained school shall on each school day take part in an act of collective worship. The arrangements for the collective worship in a school… may provide for a single act of worship for all pupils or for separate acts of worship for pupils in different age groups or in different school groups… In the case of a county school[2] *the collective worship required in the school... shall be wholly or mainly of a broadly Christian character.*

Collective worship is of a broadly Christian character if it reflects the broad traditions of Christian belief without being distinctive of any particular Christian denomination. Every act of collective worship need not comply with the above provided that, taking any school term as a whole, most such acts which take place in the school do comply with it.

EDUCATION REFORM ACT 1988: RELIGIOUS EDUCATION, SECTION 6, §§1–2;
SECTION 7 §§1–3

In simple terms this means that:

- The school community should meet for collective worship every day.
- Collective worship may take place with the whole school together or in smaller groups.
- The majority of the worship will reflect Christian belief in its widest sense, but the beliefs of other faith communities within our predominantly Christian culture can also be acknowledged and celebrated.

So what does 'broadly Christian' mean? Every school will interpret it differently. Beliefs and practices that are common to all Christians, such as Bible reading, are acceptable, but practices that are denominational, such as saying the 'Hail Mary' or teaching about infant baptism, must be avoided. The words used and the activities taking place during collective worship will recognise the existence and presence of God. (For example, a prayer that starts 'Thank you for...' raises the question of whom we are thanking.) It is wise, however, to avoid terms like 'Jesus Christ our Lord' or songs about personal discipleship, which imply that the people taking part are all committed Christian believers.

Schools have become far more secular recently, so, if helpers are going to be participating in any collective worship, they should always seek advice from the head teacher, RE coordinator or person responsible for collective worship about what is appropriate in that particular school. If possible, they should attend an act of worship beforehand.

Worship in Christian schools

The situation is different and far simpler in Church schools. The governing body has responsibility for seeing that a daily act of worship is delivered and that it is held according to the doctrine and practice of the particular Christian denomination.

Organisation of collective worship

A common pattern for collective worship is for the whole school to meet once or twice a week, with other worship being held in class or year groups. In some schools, the hall is too small to accommodate the whole school, so it will meet in key stages or year groups for worship. Collective worship is difficult to lead with a large age range that includes staff and sometimes parents, so it is preferable to have smaller age groups on some days.

Most schools will have 'class assemblies' and children are becoming increasingly involved in leading them. They usually write their own material, including the prayers, and develop skills like planning, working as a team and speaking in front of a large number of people. Parents are often invited, and their attendance gives them an insight into their children's school lives and enables them to join in their celebrations. A well-planned class act of worship brings fresh faces and ideas to the forefront, so it can be of great benefit to the whole school.

Responsibility and accountability

The ultimate responsibility for collective worship in non-church schools lies with the head teacher, although many schools appoint someone to have overall responsibility for it. Leading an act of worship is often a shared responsibility in a school. Some clergy are trained teachers who teach in a school, alongside other members of the staff, as part of their church-based ministry. Others are non-stipendiary ministers, lay preachers or Sunday school leaders who are used to leading worship at their own churches. For example, in one school, the chaplain writes a class worship programme, 'Pause for Thought', which the class tutors deliver under his guidance.

All acts of worship have to be planned and recorded. They form part of the Ofsted inspection, although faith schools have their worship inspected by their own trained and registered inspectors. Most schools follow a set of themes that last a week or fortnight, providing staff, visitors and pupils with a starting point for planning. Visitors are sometimes invited to lead a particular act of worship or to speak during it, possibly about something of national or local importance or about an aspect of their work that links with the theme. For example, a community primary school in Essex planned its programme around fortnightly themes. The local Methodist minister always led one act of worship to give a specifically Christian perspective to the theme.

Best practice in leading collective worship

An act of worship starts as the first person enters the room and ends after the last person has left it. The atmosphere should be tranquil but with a sense of expectancy. The space needs to be prepared so that there is no banging of chairs or unnecessary noise. If adults walk and speak calmly and slowly, their example will do much to encourage the children to do the same. Quiet music will help to set the scene. An act of worship can start with a greeting, a song or a symbolic act, such as lighting a candle, opening the Bible or reading from a storybook.

An inner-city primary school was in two Victorian buildings with a busy road between them. Getting over 300 children into the hall for 'whole school worship' every Monday was a logistical nightmare. Teachers got stressed and the children responded accordingly. To address this positively, the pianist invented a 'rite of gathering'. As the first class appeared, she started a repetitive song or hymn. The children joined in and each class took up the singing as they entered the hall. The class nearest the piano took her lead with the words. If any children paused for a break or whispered, the singing covered them. As the last class sat down, the pianist murmured, 'Hum', and the whole school hummed the melody, creating a silence out of the sound.

Posture and delivery

It is helpful to write out the act of worship and then reduce it to a series of points or headings. You could memorise your talk under key words, so that eye contact can be maintained and both hands are free. Alternatively, a prompt card could be used, showing the main points.

Everything should always be rehearsed. It is best to stand in a relaxed way, head up and looking towards the back of the room. We often speak too fast when we are nervous, so it is important to remember to speak clearly and slowly, and not to drop the voice at the end of sentences. Visitors should look pleased to be there and show that they enjoy leading acts of worship. Natural enthusiasm can be very infectious, so, if the speaker enjoys worshipping God, the chances are that the children will pick up something of that enjoyment.

Starting and finishing

The first words or actions will set the scene for the act of worship. Some leaders will use an action song or a game to involve the children. Visual aids or some kind of action will be more memorable than a lot of talking. Visitors should bring an object to show to the children. This item could be hidden somewhere in the room, with two children being asked to find it by following directions, or it could be placed in a 'feely bag' to encourage participation. Not all games used in children's clubs are suitable for collective worship, however. Anything that involves making a mess or clearing up should be saved for another time and place.

Another way of starting a talk is with suspense. 'I never thought I would hear that song again!' could be more effective than 'I am going to tell you about a pop song that I liked when I was at school 30 years ago and heard again last week…'

The last words will be what the children take away with them. It is helpful to finish with a 'sending out' prayer for the day, or one that draws together the subject of the worship. Creating an atmosphere where everyone has an opportunity to sense the presence of God, and then to move on to the day's work, will also be effective.

Programmes

There are numerous excellent assembly programmes, some of which are listed on the website www.barnabasinschools.org.uk. They can, of course, be adapted or used as springboards for your own ideas rather than being followed slavishly.

Instead of reading straight from the Bible, the story could be retold in the speaker's own words, or rewritten in a contemporary context. The parables were stories about everyday people and situations that Jesus' listeners would have recognised. Bible stories should be kept alive in a similar way.

Some schools use the SEAL (Social and Emotional Attitudes to Learning) programme or the scheme of 'values education'. These programmes are intended to be followed up in lesson time and, in some ways, they develop further the whole area of PSHE.[3] Other schools may use programmes produced by the local authority or diocese. In Church schools, the themes may be linked to the Christian year or parts of the Bible.

Storytelling

The Bible and other holy books are an intrinsic part of worship. They tell the story of God's relationship with creation and about the people who have been part of that relationship. They also attempt to explain through story the nature and acts of God, which are in themselves inexplicable. It is good practice to use a version of the Bible that is appropriate for the children's ages and to be prepared to alter any ambiguous or inappropriate words. The narrative should be read as you would read any other story. Using the Bible creatively with visual aids, drama and poems, such as rap or songs, will bring the story to life.

When reading from a book, the speaker should still make eye contact with the children and address the reading directly to them. It is very easy to use visual aids, showing the pictures from the book with a small group, or using whiteboards or overhead projectors with larger groups. Careful use of the tone of voice, timing, pace and movement can take the children on a journey in their own imagination that will stay with them for a long time.

The speaker's posture and actions should illustrate the words of the story—for example, walking across the room as the character goes on a journey; sitting or standing when the character does; drooping the head and speaking slowly when the character is tired or sad, and so on.

Music

Music in school worship has evolved alongside a huge expansion of hymns and worship songs, instrumental playing and high-quality recorded music. Music on a CD is often used to set the scene for collective worship, but many pupils and staff are capable musicians and are happy to play a piece during the worship, celebrating the school's many talents. Recorders and percussion instruments can be used during singing. Songs with actions, choruses or repetition are most effective, as they do not require young children to read fluently. Not every school has a member of staff who can play a piano or a guitar but children often sing better with a strong adult singer or a single melody instrument to accompany them.

The choice of hymns and songs is important. Some are best avoided because their message is unclear or they assume a level of personal commitment that is inappropriate, especially in multi-cultural situations. Others tell stories or celebrate awe and wonder in a more inclusive way. It is best to look for straightforward melodies, usually with short lines and some repetition, and try to have a mixture of styles with both traditional and modern texts. Many children love imagery and poetry, and will come to understand the meaning behind some well-known hymns as they develop linguistically and spiritually.

Prayers

Unlike church services and club meetings, most school acts of worship are compulsory and will include children of all faiths and none. It is important to try to use the language of invitation in a way that is welcoming, so that nobody feels marginalised by what should be an inclusive activity. For example, we might say, 'Listen to the words of this (Christian) prayer and make it your own if you wish.'

Schools are generally happy with using the name of 'God' in collective worship. Most people have an idea of what is meant by it. However, each school is unique and will attempt to provide worship in its own particular context. If there is any doubt about appropriate language, it is best to ask for guidance. Better still, attend an act of worship before the day and ask any questions that may arise from it at the time.

The situation is different in Church schools. The act of worship will be Christian worship in line with the tradition and practices of the particular denomination. The school may, however, contain children and staff of other faiths, and a visitor needs to be aware of this.

■ The chief Rabbi, Jonathan Sacks, speaking on BBC's *Thought for the Day* in 2008, spoke of how he learned tolerance and respect for other religions as a child when he was a pupil at a Church primary school. ■

One increasingly popular form of prayer, especially in small groups, is to help children to think spiritually, through an open-ended, meditative approach to a Bible passage or story. This format is likely to end with a question, such as, 'I wonder which part of this story was the most important for you?' or, 'I wonder what you would have said or done if you were that person?' This sort of prayer can lead to a range of more inclusive approaches than traditional praying can, and encourages pupils to feel a sense of ownership of their prayers and of the presence of God.

Using volunteers

Children enjoy helping. Many youngsters are very good at using AVA equipment, but they should always be rehearsed beforehand so that they know exactly what they need to do. If the visitor asks for volunteers during the act of worship for some kind of activity, the children should be chosen carefully. Ideally, one of the teachers should be asked to choose the child. That will remove any possible embarrassment or concerns.

If any kind of competitive activity is used, it is important to ensure that all the players are applauded. It takes a lot of courage for a child to stand up in front of everyone, so each child should get a clap for being willing to take part, rather than just being the winner. Occasionally, a visitor may include a child who is incapable of joining in fully, through disability or nervousness. It is even more important that this child feels that their effort was valued.

Visitors contributing to collective worship

Even confident and experienced teachers can feel daunted when it comes to leading an act of worship with the whole school. The age range can span from five to 65, and the worship is expected to be a memorable experience and a positive start to the day for everyone. Some teachers may feel ill at ease because the idea of worshipping God does not come easily to them. For these reasons and many others, visitors are usually welcomed into school to take part in worship, either by giving a talk about a special subject or because they are from a church or other faith community and have become involved in the life of the school.

Getting to know the school

Clergy, schools' workers and youth and children's workers often see their role in a school as being principally in the fields of worship and RE. Other Christians who are governors or parents may also get involved. Before volunteering their services, however, all helpers should start to connect with the school. For example, it would be helpful to attend some events, perhaps along with friends or family members who have children at the school, to get the 'feel' of the place and think about what time or skills they can offer. This applies especially to ministers or children's workers who are new to the area: they should ask if they can spend time in the school, getting to know the staff and children.[4]

Before offering to help with an act of worship, we should remember that:

- Leading worship requires skill and practice.
- The easiest worship to lead is a formal service with a strong structure. Collective worship in school will not necessarily have any particular structure.
- Worship with mixed age groups is difficult. Each person needs to be offered an opportunity to give and receive in worship in his or her own way.
- Collective worship in a school is not the same as worship in a church service or in a youth club.
- This may be the only act of worship that some of the children and adults will ever experience.

So the big word is 'preparation'! A good way to start could be to offer some kind of help with a single act of worship, on a theme or subject that is of particular interest to an individual. For example, there may be someone in the church who could talk about their involvement with a charity or a local project. If someone has a skill, such as music, they might be able to teach or lead some singing.

Similarly, it may be possible to have input to a particular lesson or class worship. The children will be pleased to welcome visitors to their classroom and get to know them. There will be about 30 children of similar age, so the contribution should be easier to plan. Opportunities to participate may come from the most unexpected places and may not necessarily be directly connected with an act of worship. For example, in one school, the Science coordinator approached a retired biologist who collected his granddaughter from school occasionally. The child had said that her grandfather had solar heating, so would he be willing to tell her class about it? The Science coordinator visited the grandfather's house to see the solar heating in operation and discussed how it could be incorporated into a particular lesson. This was a great success, and the class later used the information imaginatively in their worship for harvest.

Planning

As soon as the date is in the diary, visitors should start work by jotting down ideas, quotes, possible visual aids and even whole phrases to be used in the talk, as the ideas occur to them. It is a less stressful and more effective way of working to keep a running list than to try to think of everything at the last minute. Any ideas not used in the first talk can be saved for another time.

Plenty of time should be given to thinking about how to use elements from the children's world—for example, where they live, their interests, music, TV, computer games and so on. Clips from DVDs can be useful, but the clip needs to be viewed several times and an introduction carefully prepared. The visitor may have seen the film lots of times, but it may be totally unfamiliar to some of the children. Something from the children's culture should be used to lead to the message of the worship. That way, the speaker will have gained the children's interest and will be able to sustain it.

It is important to remember that collective worship in school comes from an educational perspective, not an evangelistic one. We are Christians leading worship, but, even if we are in a Church school, we must not proselytise or encourage children to come to a particular church.

Thorough research could include:

- A conversation with the class teacher, RE coordinator or person responsible for collective worship.
- Attending an act of worship to see how it is run. Visitors should not be afraid to say that they want to present their talk in a certain way, and should guard against being pressurised into doing something with less preparation than they think is necessary.
- Establishing the age range and abilities of the children, including any with particular difficulties or special needs.
- Asking how much time has been allocated and how the speaker's input will slot in with the rest of the act of worship.
- Deciding what resources will be needed and checking well in advance if AVA equipment or particular furniture can be made available.
- Asking for suggestions of a song to go with the theme. If the speaker can offer a suggestion, the teacher may find time to revise the song or teach it to the children.

Facing a large number of children and staff to lead a whole act of worship can feel intimidating. That is understandable, but there is an advantage in not having to fit around other people's contributions. Again, the secret is in the planning. Visitors should never attempt to fluff through a subject that they do not know thoroughly. It is important to be well-informed and, if unsure about something, to find out about it. Children cannot be conned and they deserve the best teaching and acts of worship possible.

Challenges to be worked around

Always check beforehand that there will be enough teachers present to offer support during collective worship. Visitors are not covered by the school's insurance to take responsibility for pupils and should never have to sort out behavioural issues or ask for information about the way the school operates. Ideally, the member of staff who invited the visitor should be present to introduce him or her to the children.

Notices, discipline issues or the presentation of merit certificates can squeeze the time available for the talk or act of worship. It is advisable for the speaker to ask the person who has invited them what else will be happening and how long they will have for their contribution. In practice, there is usually less time than expected because of the time taken in getting children into the hall. In a primary school, 10–20 minutes is a good guide.

It is important never to run over the time allocated. This can affect sports, music lessons, outside visits, tests and television programmes as well as normal lessons. Visitors will not be thanked by anyone for contributing to these kinds of difficulties.

On the day, visitors need to:

• Pray for the school and for God's guidance in the church's work there.
• Arrive early enough to set up and test any resources.
• See that everything is ready before the first class enters the hall.
• Take a moment on their own to compose themselves.
• Keep a record of what they did for future reference.

A final thought

Leading an act of worship in a school isn't for everyone, and there are many other ways in which someone can contribute to the life of a school. If people feel that they should lead worship because they are ordained and for no other reason, if they are terrified by leading worship with children, or if they fear that they have never led worship well, then they should not do it!

7

School as a praying community

One Friday morning the staff and children arrived at school to find that an arsonist had set fire to the building during the night. Everything was blackened. Glass had cracked in the heat; the children's work and the school's pets had been destroyed. The next morning, children, staff, parents, governors and members of the community assembled at the church next door for a first Holy Communion service. The church was packed. In the midst of the shock and loss, the automatic response was to turn to God for comfort and to support the young people on their special day.

'We are a Christian community. If it happens, it includes worship.' This description by the assistant head teacher of a secondary school in Dorset gives a brief image of a school that is a praying community. It is about more than having well-prepared and imaginative collective worship or a particular scheme of RE. It is about being rooted in a Christian ethos, where worship permeates everything that the school is and does. This chapter will unpack many of the ways in which schools live out the Christian ethos with prayer at the heart, but it is not necessarily about being a 'Church school' with particular policies. A small group of staff, governors or parents who live out their faith and pray regularly for any school can have a transforming effect on its life.

■ In an inner London primary school in the mid 1980s, about 75 per cent of the staff were committed Christians who lived out their faith in their work. While respecting the multicultural intake of the school, they worked hard to promote an ethos of valuing and caring for each child, insisting on courtesy and mutual respect. Many of the children lived in substandard accommodation including 'bed and breakfast'; a few were recent immigrants with all the challenges that these situations present, but the atmosphere of the school was warm and calm. Bad behaviour was treated with concern for a child who had a need to be addressed, rather than a 'naughty child'. Attendance was excellent; fighting was rare and bullying unknown. Children with 'difficulties' were often sent to the school from other schools. At the time, there was a tendency to treat religious belief as something personal for the committed few and remove it from school life. The school bucked the trend and took a great deal of trouble to include and celebrate the varied faiths and cultures in its worship.

Much of this was achieved by having a first-class stable staff, and the principles on which the school was run should be those of any school. It is not without significance, however, that the school was prayed for regularly in several local churches and by many staff and parents. One teacher with a difficult class said that she always prayed as she walked to school, 'Lord, make me kind to those children!' A local clergyman commented that he wished he had such a Christian community (in the broadest sense) in his own Church school.

The practicalities of the following examples and suggestions depend on the situation of the individual school. Some suggestions, however, like setting up a parents' prayer group, can take place anywhere, and every church can pray for its local schools and let them know that they have done so.

Prayer in the classroom

Praying as a class is different from formal collective worship, although it may replace collective worship on several days of the week. The children in a class are of similar age and spend most of every day together, working and playing. They will have strong friendship bonds. Issues that arise will relate to this close-knit group and they will be praying in the familiar surroundings of their own classroom.

Some classrooms have set aside a special worship area. This can be as simple as a corner or alcove with cushions and a display. It can also be used as a quiet corner where children may go at any time. Pastel colours are sometimes used to give a sense of tranquillity. Some teachers involve the children in helping to design or look after the area. If there is not enough space in the classroom for a designated worship area, some teachers will make a display or focal point for prayer. A primary school in Sussex has a brightly coloured canopy set up in one classroom. When the children meet for prayer, it is lowered slightly to create a 'prayer tent' and the children sit beneath it. Focal points include a cross, a picture on the wall or a display relating to the theme of the week's collective worship. Coloured material or paintings are also used in some classrooms to reflect the theme—for example, green for creation and life, gold for kingship, red for power and so on.

Preparing a lively class for prayer starts by creating a calm atmosphere—speaking deliberately and quietly, moving slowly to encourage calmness, or sitting quietly. Lighting a candle before prayer helps children to focus. The person leading the worship could explain that, for Christians, the light of a candle is a reminder that Jesus said he was the light for the world. Quiet recorded music, a short song or a saying, such as 'Jesus said, "I am the light for the world"' as a candle is lit, will set the scene.

Prayers should be short and simple. For example, the children may sit quietly in a group on the floor and say out loud what they want to thank God for, which might include events at home or school, celebrations and also small things, like new shoes. They can be invited to remember good things in the wider world that they have seen on television. After a short pause, they can then be encouraged to say what they want to tell God about—for example, people they love, family illness, poverty, world famine, children who are absent and so on. Finally, the children could pray for the whole world before sitting in silence for a few seconds, offering their prayers to God and then finishing by saying the Lord's Prayer together.

Special situations

Every so often, an item of national importance will be announced during the school day. This may be a time of great celebration, like the announcement that London had been awarded the 2012 Olympics, or news that prisoners have been found safe and released from their captors. Other national events may cause sadness or horror. War may seem very remote from us, but not if a child has a relative in the Armed Forces. Events involving the death or disappearance of a child may cause children to worry about their own safety. Local news will raise the same issues.

Personal and academic achievements are causes for thanksgiving. Serious illness and bereavement are times when the community can gather to pray for the person affected, his or her family and themselves at a time of loss.

It may occasionally be appropriate to bring the school together for an announcement and prayers, but more often the class can spend a few moments praying together at the end of the day. Alternatively, the particular news can be included in the next day's worship. The National Society's website[1] has an excellent section of prayers and reflections for small groups on almost any subject, for any age and season.

The death of a child or member of staff will inevitably have a devastating effect on a school community. Every school will have a different way of handling a difficult situation of this kind. The local church and clergy can prove valuable support, but this will come out of a long-term relationship of trust.[2]

Quiet spaces

Some schools set apart an area to be a quiet space. In a Church school, this can be similar in layout to the worship area in a classroom, but it will have a slightly different function. It will be open to anyone who wants to go there to be quiet or to pray at any time. It will illustrate the Christian nature of the school. A few schools will make the space into a chapel. This may be a designated room or an area off the hall or a corridor, rather like a library area. If a school decides to use space in this way, it needs to be decorated and maintained well, as it will show how the school community regards worship. Furnishings and displays need to be easy to maintain; a plain cross, a painted Salvadorean cross or an open Bible could be the main features. Posters with biblical texts or a display of flowers, glass and pebbles can help to focus the mind. Plain fabrics in the colours of the Christian year also help to set the scene.[3] Cushions or low stools are probably the best type of seating.

Prayer groups and networks

Some schools may have a prayer group meeting regularly during a lunch hour in a classroom or in the quiet place. This can include parents and governors as well as the staff and pupils. An interesting all-age prayer group was set up at a primary school near Market Harborough in Leicestershire by a parent, who had been the Chair of governors.

■ I had initially suggested that we had a prayer network where adults met to pray for the school, but then we decided to meet at school and thought it only right that the children should be welcome. It is now a lunchtime activity for the children and the children easily outnumber the adults. I took part in an assembly to introduce the idea and we had a box for the children to put in prayer requests. This worked to start with, but we gradually moved away from it. Now I turn up on a Thursday at 12.30pm. The lunchtime supervisor blows the whistle and shouts, 'Prayer Network' and the children run in: usually about 15 of varying ages. We sometimes sing 'Thank you, Lord, for this fine day' but replace the verses with our own words, seeing if we can remember each person's 'thank you' thing as we go around the circle. Other prayers use actions so everyone is doing something the whole time. We always end with a prayer adapted from Numbers 6:24, 'May the Lord bless us and keep us'.

Less formal prayer networks can be formed by a group of people agreeing to pray for the school on a particular day or time. Any particular subjects for prayer can be circulated as they arise. Direct contact or a phone conversation is the best way to communicate prayer requests. The use of email is best avoided if the subject is sensitive, and confidentiality should always be maintained about any information of a personal nature.

Church prayers

Local churches as well as individuals can support the school with their prayers. The school can also pray for a church on special occasions, such as an anniversary of dedication or patronal festival, or if a vicar or minister is leaving or a new one being appointed.

When a class visits a church, it is easy to forget that the building is principally a house of prayer. A cathedral education officer commented that one of the most frequently asked questions was, 'Do you still have services?' Her answer, 'Yes, three a day, and at least one with music', caused surprise and encouraged the visitors to think again about the current use of the building, rather than just looking at its history. A school visit to a church could be concluded with some space for quiet and a short prayer. This provides a valuable link with the worshipping community as well as the people who have come to the church to worship God over the years—for baptisms, weddings and funerals, as well as to bring all their hopes and fears.[4]

Sometimes children could be invited to visit a church to say a prayer for a special reason. This encourages them to be familiar with the building as well as finding it natural to go there to pray.

A vicar in Kent invited local children and their parents to pop into the church after school on Fridays during Lent to say or write a prayer. He put up a large whiteboard with some felt-tipped pens in the chancel. And the children came! Every week the board was covered with prayers. The youngest children offered brightly coloured drawings. Older children wrote neatly in black.

Helping local churches

A school can support a church by offering to take a special act of worship. This can be as big as transferring a school Eucharist or special service to the church on the following Sunday, perhaps for Mothering Sunday or Harvest Thanksgiving, with the children leading most of the service. Christmas is a pressurised time for everyone, but a school choir or a class could provide a short service, sing a couple of carols or perform a nativity play that has already been performed in school.

Taking a service, music or drama to a church or anywhere else requires a lot of organisation and good will from families, but it can be a very real way of supporting a local church and strengthening the prayerful relationship between the two communities. Whatever the effort, it is always rewarded by the confidence it gives to the children as they use their talents and share worship with others.

A final thought

As well as being influenced by the example and enthusiasm of their children, some parents who attend worship at their children's school have themselves been educated in a Christian school or have been to church or Sunday school as children. Joining in an act of worship in a familiar building and a relaxed atmosphere leads some of them to revisit their faith and ask questions.

*

8

The Eucharist in school

We were initially very sceptical about offering Communion, but in the end this is what made the day! Each school's contribution to the service in the form of liturgical dance, drama, prayer or music was truly an act of worship, not merely entertainment— many of the items were very moving and thought-provoking. What a wonderful Spirit-filled experience to mark the end of the pupils' time at a Church school.

ROCHESTER CATHEDRAL'S EDUCATION OFFICERS

A school is not just a building designed for children's education. It is a community in its own right with opportunities for daily collective worship, a place where each child's spiritual development is considered to be part of his or her education as whole people. These opportunities include corporate worship with children, staff, parents and governors taking part.

Nearly a million children attend Church of England schools and about 500,000 attend Roman Catholic schools. 'Going to Mass' is deeply embedded in the Roman Catholic ethos and every Roman Catholic school will have eucharistic worship as a matter of course. In 2005, about half of Church of England schools held eucharistic worship at some time and the number is increasing. Christian teachers have seen how including children in the Eucharist at their own churches has enriched their worship, so they want to take the same experience into their schools.

Diocesan schools' festivals may end with a Eucharist. With experience, schools have become less fearful and clergy more confident as they find ways of making it a creative and inclusive celebration. A rough estimate is that about a million children in total will attend a Eucharist at school at some time. The question is:

are they simply 'present', or are they taking part in a creative act of worship where they meet Jesus, present in his word and sacrament, and allow the experience to transform their lives and the life of their school community?

Changes in the composition of our society, as well as within church traditions, have raised the profile and numbers of Christian children receiving Holy Communion. The pattern in the major denominations is varied:

- The Orthodox Church has always given Holy Communion at the same time as baptism. Most baptismal candidates are babies or very young children.
- The Roman Catholic Church usually admits children to Holy Communion at 7–8 years, and has been doing so since the late 19th century.
- The Methodist Church issued guidelines for admission of children to Holy Communion in 1987. This is now official policy.
- The Church of England issued guidelines in 1997 to allow children to receive Holy Communion with the bishop's permission. These became regulations in 2006.
- It is becoming increasingly common for churches in the Church of Scotland and the United Reformed Church to admit baptised children to Holy Communion before the age of confirmation or membership.

With this situation, as well as the increasing numbers of children from different Christian cultures living in Britain, we can assume that a large number of Church schools will have communicant children as well as adults. Linking these movements with the more consciously Christian ethos of most Church schools, many head teachers, chairs of governors or clergy have asked questions like, 'Should our leavers' service (or other special event) be a Eucharist?' or 'Can we have a Eucharist in school?' And many have answered, 'Yes!'

■ The diocese of Rochester had always had an act of worship at its schools' festivals, with each school producing an item for the concluding act of worship, but three years ago it decided to have a Eucharist instead. Jan Thompson, the schools' officer, wrote: 'The themes we have used so far have been "remembering" and "thanksgiving", giving the opportunity to explore the theme's connection with the Eucharist as well as its relevance in the lives of the pupils. Pupils still make their creative contributions to the service—their procession of banners, music-making, singing, readings, drama and liturgical dance—but this is held together within a more structured act of worship. There is also more opportunity for everyone to participate throughout the whole service, as they follow the words of the service and join in with the responses. At the Offertory, a basket is taken up with prayers written by pupils in the interactive prayer sessions in the morning, and each school offers a scrapbook of Year 6's memories of their school. When the sacrament is distributed, everyone either receives it (if they do so in their own church), has a personal blessing, or just walks by.' ■

Schools and churches are gradually moving away from the old style of service. It is no longer something that the priest does to a passive congregation; instead the priest presides over the school community as they make Eucharist together. He or she can say the opening greeting, leaving the children to introduce the service and lead a 'sorry' prayer, which they may have written themselves. Similarly, the presiding minister may introduce and end the Gospel reading, while the children read or act it out in their own way. Children will serve, provide music, write and lead prayers, read from the Bible and teach through art and drama. It is their service.

Common Worship,[1] while not a perfect solution, has given freedom to experiment though its numerous options. This has led to less fear of using material from other traditions or adapting texts for particular situations. Eucharistic prayers to be used when children are present are in preparation and should be published in 2010.[2]

A primary school had close links with its church over a number of years. Its worship was centred on the weekly Eucharist for the whole school, when the vicar presided. The service was identical to a weekday service in the church. The vicar said all the prayers and read the readings for the day, while the children and staff said the responses and joined in the Lord's Prayer. Only the vicar and head teacher received Holy Communion.

A few miles away, another primary school prepared for its termly Eucharist. It was July and the theme was 'moving on'. The children who were leaving to go to secondary school had chosen the songs and produced a display of work on the theme. They had written about their feelings, painted pictures about journeys and displayed a map with their new schools marked on it and a huge new school bag. They read the prayers and readings, the choir led the music and two of the staff helped to administer Holy Communion. Every person received either Holy Communion or a blessing. Each Year 6 child was given a Bible as a leaving present from the school.

The above case studies raise three closely linked points: frequency, manner and experience. Both of these schools valued the Eucharist highly as an intrinsic part of their worship but expressed it in different ways.

Frequency

Many schools have a weekly or fortnightly Eucharist and see it as part of the rhythm of the week. It includes the staff and perhaps some parents and governors. Others have a termly or annual celebration to mark a special event. Some schools have eucharistic services for year groups or individual classes. They have a strong sense of community and are often easier to lead than a service for a whole school of different ages and backgrounds. A few offer voluntary eucharistic services during the lunch hour or after school for anyone who wants to attend.

Manner

The manner in which the service is celebrated should not reflect a kind of worship that is 'done' to the children, but should offer an act in which they can take a full part, some more obviously than others. The importance of the service is shown by the care that is taken with it, but it need not be elaborate or time-consuming. The worship in the second case study above drew together work that was already being done and offered it to God. By arranging for each class to take responsibility in turn, a school could offer the same sort of Eucharist more frequently. The extra preparation needed is minimal, but every person is involved in some way and has an opportunity to experience a sense of the presence of God. For neglected or abused children, a hand on the head and a simple, 'May the Lord Jesus bless you' may be the only accepting touch and prayer they ever receive.

Experience

'How can I make Jesus real to the children?' asked a despairing head teacher on a wet Friday afternoon. There are no quick and easy answers to a question like that, but perhaps the disciple Andrew's 'Come and see' is a start. Children (and adults) meet Jesus in a number of ways, and one way is through other people. Some people have a real inherent goodness and even the most reprobate child or hardened atheist will sense it.

Beyond the worship

The Eucharist has many facets, including an educational element. Every school will find different ways of putting the curriculum and worship together.

Use of the creative arts

A huge amount of suitable music can be used in worship. The basic form of the Eucharist is always the same so children can learn to sing a simple setting, and most children enjoy singing if it is led well and becomes part of their lives. A lot of Christian teaching can be done through hymns and carols. Instruments can be included, such as simple percussion, as a group or a solo. Staff and children can also perform together—a powerful demonstration of how all contributions can be valued, no matter what one's age.

Children can explore a theme or season through art and craft, and their work can be displayed in the church or school for the service. For example, a Eucharist for Pentecost can include painting in 'fire' colours by the youngest children. Older pupils can produce more descriptive pictures; they could also make wind chimes or even kites.

Bible passages can be read in parts, mimed or acted out. This is more memorable than having just one person simply reading. A group could act a play based on the reading or provide a short drama that provides teaching on the subject. If there is space, a dance for the Gloria, at the Offertory or as thanksgiving after Communion can be very effective. Prayers with actions help people to join in and make the prayers their own: actions speak louder than words.

Teaching on special services, signs and symbols

Eucharistic services in schools can become a catalyst for exploring the other sacraments. As the Eucharist became established in one school, a pattern of teaching evolved. The Reception class studied baptism. Some children would find this familiar as they would have seen younger siblings and relatives baptised. They heard the story of John the Baptist baptising Jesus (Matthew 3:13–17). They asked their parents about their own baptisms and brought mementos—certificates, Bibles, photographs and presents—to school. They learned about the service and had a doll's 'baptism' in church, with a party and cake afterwards.

In Year 1 they moved on to marriage. The teaching led to acting out a wedding in church, with the children taking every part: there were guests wearing hats and a child playing the part of the vicar. The 'bride' and her 'father' were driven across the road by a parent with a large car. The parents came to the service and they had a wedding reception afterwards.

Children in Year 2 attended the local church Eucharist to celebrate their school's birthday. Teaching focused on the last supper, crucifixion and resurrection of Jesus, and the importance of being a worshipping community. Children in Year 3 and above were involved in the twice-termly eucharistic services, so this teaching was ongoing. Ash Wednesday was always kept with a Eucharist for Key Stage 2 children and a service in school for Key Stage 1. Part of the preparation for this event was teaching on reconciliation.

Living the Eucharist in daily life

If a school's eucharistic life is to make sense, there is an obvious consequence: the adults have to live it out in everything they do and help the children through the example of their own lives, just as much as in their formal teaching. Respect and compassion for all should therefore be part of the 'hidden curriculum' of any school that stands by the values embodied in celebrating a Eucharist.

Listening to God's word in the Bible readings leads to listening to children and helping them listen to each other. Prayers for the world, neighbours and people in need must be lived out. One way to do this is by arranging for the school or a class to have links with a particular charity and encouraging the children to live out their prayers among their families and the people they meet in their daily lives.

Prayers for those who are unwell or in need can be put into practice by visiting a friend in hospital or making a card for a relative who is ill. Remembering refugees and people who are lonely can be put into practice by helping a child who is new to the class or offering to play with someone who is alone.

Sharing the Peace is a time for starting again, for putting aside fights or quarrels. It is about respecting each other and those in authority. Offering bread and wine is about offering everything that we have and valuing God's goodness to us, which includes respecting the environment and sharing God's gifts with people who are less well off. The dismissal is about living out the Christian life in our school and our home, with our family and with our friends.

Being inclusive

A school Eucharist can turn on their head any preconceived ideas that the children might not be suitable to take part in eucharistic worship, or that a service geared towards children is somehow inferior. It can be truly an all-age service, some children being communicants and some adults being blessed. A child of seven may say the prayer for forgiveness, and a teaching assistant may administer Holy Communion. A pupil with learning difficulties may offer his or her work at the Offertory while an exceptionally talented musician plays the flute. The vicar or minister may only contribute to the parts of the service where a priest is needed and the head teacher will be able to sit quietly at the back.

Ideally, a school Eucharist will be a truly all-age celebration in which everyone can participate, whatever their age and stage of faith. However, a school may rightly be concerned about children of different faiths and certainly those of none. There are no easy answers but the following case studies show how two schools attempted to address situations that arose quite suddenly.

An inner-city Roman Catholic secondary school held its usual 'Welcome Mass' for the Year 7 students and their parents in November. Another local secondary school had been closed and they suddenly found that about 60 per cent of the new students were from other faiths or Christian traditions. For the first Bible reading they took the text, 'In the future, the mountain with the Lord's temple will be the highest of all. It will reach above the hills; every nation will rush to it. Many people will come and say, "Let's go to the mountain of the Lord God of Jacob and worship in his temple"' (Isaiah 2:2–3). This was to show how all nations and cultures will move towards God from their different directions. A huge map was displayed. Students pointed to their ancestral homelands and said the words, 'Let's go to the mountain of the Lord' in their mother tongues. Six Hindu girls did a dance for Diwali at the Offertory. Everyone was offered a blessing, which was 'God bless you,' and many accepted the invitation. There was a party afterwards.

In a school in Dorset, a 16-year-old student died after a long illness. His class met to discuss what sort of service should be held to remember him. It was eventually agreed that, because he had been a communicant, it should be held in the context of Holy Communion. This raised an issue, however. Not all of the class members were Christians, let alone communicants. How could this service be made truly inclusive so that every person felt involved? They decided to follow the Orthodox tradition of offering blessed bread. This was made by some of the students in a cookery lesson and handed to everyone at the end of the service. ■

A school where members live their faith, where faith is part of the whole ethos rather than a chore, and is not used as a put-down ('If you behave like that, you shouldn't be in a Christian school'), will have an effect that percolates through the community in time and influences innumerable young lives.[3] Eucharistic worship is an intrinsic part of that experience. Getting to that position will take time, however, and has to start with a vision. It is risky, but, with careful preparation and support, it will work and can transform the whole school. Practices will need to be constantly reviewed, as with all aspects of the school's life, as situations change. If we wait until everything is 'right', we will wait for ever.

A final thought

Today's culture of competition and individual success from an early age has done much to diminish the joy of taking part, of being part of a team. We may want to encourage healthy competition and reward excellence, but it can go too far. Then life becomes composed of winners and losers—those who have and those who have not.

■ It was sports day for the Reception and Key Stage 1 classes. The Reception class lined up for their first race. The tape was stretched near enough to make the distance achievable and far enough for it to look like a race. The whistle blew and the little group set off. As with all races, one child came first, another came last and everyone else was in between. The children clustered around the winner, rosy-faced and laughing. They had all taken part; they were all happy. A mother said anxiously to her son, 'Are you disappointed that you didn't win?' The little boy looked puzzled and then shook his head.

In a school Eucharist, everyone takes part, as in that running race. Some have special tasks, some are communicants, but they all celebrate together. Whatever their age or background, they are all loved by God and valued by their community. For a short time, SATs, targets and league tables can be set aside as the school gathers at the Lord's table to celebrate the Eucharist together.

Religious Education, PSHE and Citizenship

Religious education provokes challenging questions about the ultimate meaning and purpose of life... It develops pupils' knowledge and understanding of Christianity, other principal religions, other religious traditions and other worldviews that offer answers to questions such as these... It offers opportunities for personal reflection and spiritual development... Religious education encourages pupils to learn from different religions, beliefs, values and traditions while exploring their own beliefs and questions of meaning. It challenges pupils to reflect on, consider, analyse, interpret and evaluate issues of truth, belief, faith and ethics and to communicate their responses.

NON-STATUTORY NATIONAL FRAMEWORK FOR RELIGIOUS EDUCATION
(QCA, 2004)

The Christian faith has been widely practised in Britain for well over 1000 years and is an intrinsic part of our British heritage and culture.

The Church has been involved in children's education since the eighth century, when boys were recruited to the monasteries to help to copy the Bible and Mass books. We have read in Chapter 2 how its establishment of distinctively Christian voluntary schools eventually led to universal free education. This was followed by the Butler Education Act (1944), which made daily collective worship and Religious Education compulsory, while allowing parents the right to withdraw their children.

As we have seen, schools have changed radically since 1944 to reflect a rapidly changing society but Religious Education has remained part of every child's education. The Education Reform

Act of 1988 reiterated the importance of collective worship and RE, while including study of other religions to reflect the diversity of faiths in today's society.

Reasons for teaching RE

Religious Education used to be considered to be the main channel for moral education. It became increasingly overburdened as more and more demands were made on the timetable of one or two lessons each week. Today, schools provide teaching on human values in a variety of ways under the main headings of Personal, Social and Health Education (PSHE) and Citizenship. This has lifted a load from the RE curriculum and thus provided new opportunities to teach it as a subject in its own right.

The media occasionally suggest that all ideologies, including a religious perspective, should be removed from children's education. Education can never be value-free, however, and removing the religious dimension would leave a vacuum to be filled by a different ideology, such as nationalism or hardline secularism. Young people could be left unprepared to encounter religious belief or culture. Pupils from faith backgrounds could be made to feel that their beliefs don't matter or are not respected. This might result in feelings of isolation and even resentment towards educational institutions and society in general.

Those arguments provide only a handful of several reasons for teaching about Christianity in RE as part of every child's education, even though only a minority of the population are committed churchgoers. A more positive reason is that Christianity is part of our British make-up. Our monarchy and government are distinctively Christian. Its moral values and practice form the basis of our legal system and spirit of public service. The English language and literature are full of biblical references and Christian teaching. Many parents, whether believers or not, have a deep desire for their children to know the Christian story as part of their cultural heritage. In an article entitled 'Mummy, why are those people praying?' (*The Spectator*, December 2000), the author, a self-confessed agnostic with atheist parents, expressed concern that her children knew more about Diwali than Christmas, and that an intrinsic part of our British culture was being eroded. The government adds another reason:

Religious education makes a distinctive contribution to the school curriculum by developing pupils' knowledge and understanding of religion, religious beliefs, practices, language and traditions and their influence on individuals, communities, societies and cultures. It enables pupils to consider and respond to a range of important questions related to their own spiritual development, the development of values and attitudes and fundamental questions concerning the meaning and purpose of life.

QUALIFICATIONS AND CURRICULUM AUTHORITY, 2000

RE today

So, what is RE really like in today's schools? The quick answer is that it is alive and well. Every school has to teach RE. Parents have the right to withdraw their children but this practice has become increasingly uncommon as people recognise the value to children of learning about religions and relating religious ideas to their own lives. Most schools will teach a locally agreed syllabus (see below). Teaching standards and the allocated time and funding vary, but the 2008 HMI subject inspection described the teaching in primary schools as 'stable and rarely inadequate'. A committed RE coordinator can make a great difference and some schools are deeply aware of the value of RE in developing children's spirituality and encouraging good community relationships.

At secondary level, RE is a popular subject for GCSE and AS/ A Level exams. Numbers rise every year and over two-thirds of students now gain a GCSE qualification in Religious Education or Religious Studies.

The RE curriculum

RE holds a unique place in children's education. It is compulsory but not part of the National Curriculum. Each local authority in England appoints teachers, councillors and representatives of faith communities to its Standing Advisory Council for Religious Education (SACRE), which works within a national framework to create and oversee a locally agreed syllabus.

This allows for a curriculum that can respond to the local culture and faith communities. As a result, the RE syllabus in, for example, Bradford or Birmingham has the potential to be different from that in Carlisle or Cornwall, although much of the content will be similar.

The position in Church schools is that pupils in Controlled schools will study the locally agreed syllabus, but the governing body in Aided schools may choose to have their own syllabus, based on denominational teaching and usually designed by the diocesan education department.[1]

Personal, Social and Health Education

PSHE is an important but currently non-statutory part of the primary curriculum. Many primary schools teach it because they feel that pupils benefit from learning about healthy lifestyles, managing feelings and building positive relationships. It aims to help children to understand how they develop personally and socially, as well as discussing the moral, social and cultural issues that are part of growing up.

PSHE is taught in a variety of ways but the QCA has produced joint non-statutory frameworks for Citizenship and PSHE at both KS1 and KS2, which give guidance on the sort of topics that are studied under both headings.

Children aged 5–7 years learn about:

- Themselves as individuals and as members of their communities.
- Basic rules and skills for keeping healthy and safe.
- Their feelings, views, needs and rights, and how to recognise and respect them in others.
- Taking responsibility for themselves and their environments.
- Social skills: sharing, taking turns, playing, helping others, resolving conflict.
- Recognising and resisting bullying.

Children aged 7–11 years learn about:

- Being growing and changing individuals with their own experiences and ideas.
- Being members of communities.
- Staying healthy and safe; managing risk.
- The wider world and the interdependence of communities within it.
- Social justice and moral responsibility.
- How their own choices and behaviour can affect local, national or global issues and political and social institutions.
- How to make more confident and informed choices about their health, behaviour and environment.
- Taking more responsibility, individually and as a group, for their own learning.
- Defining and resisting bullying.

Citizenship and community cohesion

Many schools already work in ways that promote awareness of the communities in which they live and encourage community cohesion. The DCSF wants every school to ensure that all pupils understand and appreciate others from different backgrounds with a sense of shared values, fulfilling their potential and feeling part of a community at a local, national and international level. This has now become mandatory and forms part of the Ofsted inspection.

As well as this curriculum, which relates to the local community, the School Linking programme helps schools to develop links with other schools in different parts of the country. On an international level, having a partner school in another country (for example, some schools in East Sussex are linked with schools in Sierra Leone) shows practical examples of how other children live, their communities and education, as well as an opportunity to discuss the distinctive heritage and culture of their countries and other issues.

The event of the 2012 Olympic Games in London also offers an ideal opportunity for schools to explore the Olympic ideals of global citizenship, sustainability and the future of the planet.

Helping with RE, PSHE and Citizenship

Members of local churches have a lot to offer to schools by helping with RE as well as contributing to discussion of human values from a faith perspective in PSHE or Citizenship lessons. For children, the effect of meeting and talking to real Christians about their beliefs and the way they live out their faith can be far stronger and longer-lasting than reading the best textbook. Visiting Christians may be members of a local church or linked to an organisation like *Open the Book* or *RE Inspired*.

■ RE Inspired offers local schools innovative Religious Education sessions, delivering units on Christianity from the school's syllabus in which pupils learn about the Christian faith from Christians in local churches. Each session is discussed with the teachers beforehand and tailored individually as needed. The sessions, which incorporate a range of learning styles, are designed and delivered by Christians from local churches— sometimes by teachers or ministers but generally by folk from the pews. They encourage the pupils to think, to ask questions, to challenge preconceived ideas and to offer them the opportunity to think, learn and respond in a spiritual way. Pupils are always told that we are not attempting to change their beliefs but to explore the topic, to learn about what it means to Christians and what the pupils can learn from studying it. ■

PAUL HAYNES RE INSPIRED PROJECT DIRECTOR

Churches can also be of great help with studies of the local community. They could provide people to talk about their paid or voluntary work as well as the contribution of the church. A church could also work with a school in forging a link with a school and church in another area or another country, with an interchange of information and possibly the provision of hospitality.

For anyone interested in helping with RE in a school, a sensible first step would be to look at a copy of the local agreed syllabus. The school should be able to give or lend a copy, or one could be obtained from the local education office. If the school is Church Aided, it may use its own syllabus, which should be available from the diocesan office. Read through it and mark any subjects in which you or another church member might have enough knowledge to provide help. This will take some time, but it will give the broader picture and show how the church can contribute within the delivery of the whole syllabus.

Similarly, with the permission and support of their minister or vicar, potential helpers could find out from the school how it teaches PSHE and Citizenship, or use the lists on page 90 as guidance, and then make a note of what they have to offer.

An approach can then be made to the RE coordinator or head teacher. If this is the church's first approach to the school, it would be helpful to include the note of skills or knowledge being offered when contacting the head teacher. For RE, refer to the local agreed syllabus, so that the head knows that the church has prepared its approach carefully.[2]

Taking part in a lesson

Once the school knows that someone from the church is available, a teacher will make contact when input is needed for a particular lesson. This may involve taking part in a lesson or helping to arrange a school visit to the church.[3]

Teaching requires both skill and stamina, so visitors need to prepare the work carefully[4] and find out whether they are expected to facilitate discussion or to give a short talk and then answer questions. If there is any doubt about what to do, it may be possible to sit in on a few lessons to see what happens or talk to someone who has helped in a similar way. Speakers should ensure that they have interesting stories to tell and objects to show. Pupils respond well to new things so visitors will have a good opportunity to make their contribution interesting and memorable to the children.

Meeting people of faith

It is easy to teach about the practices of various religions but it can be difficult for teachers to gain an appreciation of what it is like to live out one's faith as a Christian, Jew or Hindu and the effect that that particular faith community has on the wider locality. Churches and other faith communities can do much to help with developing this understanding. For example, children will learn a certain amount by listening to an account of a Christian baptism or marriage, but they will gain and retain far more by visiting a church to act out the service with a priest or minister, or by interviewing someone who has recently been baptised or married.[5]

Cross-curricular RE

There is an increasing desire in primary schools to link RE with areas of the curriculum such as literacy, history, PSHE, Citizenship and the arts. For example, a topic such as 'The meaning of Christmas' can be studied using the biblical text, then explored further through stories, explanation of historical customs, art, drama, poetry and music. There is huge potential for creative teaching, including visits or the contribution of outside visitors, which is to be welcomed. On the other hand, there is a risk that distinctive RE teaching can be diluted or almost disappear. It can also be difficult to allow parents to withdraw their children from RE lessons if it becomes entirely cross-curricular or topic-based.

■ When I started my role, I wanted to be able to go into schools and teach about the truth of Jesus' love. I made a programme now known as 'The Easter Experience', where I worked with a class for the day, presenting the Easter story from Palm Sunday to Ascension. Then the children worked in groups to perform a section of the story, which they later presented to the whole school. We also carried out craft activities. The demand is now so large and there aren't enough hours in the day, so I do sessions with classes, presenting the story in an interactive way. I have now created similar events for

Christmas and Harvest. They are so popular with the children and staff. The children always stop me in the street to ask when I am going again. ■

VOLUNTARY HELPER, MALMESBURY, WILTSHIRE

A final thought

Helpers may find that they are invited regularly to contribute to a lesson on a particular subject. They need to ensure that their material is kept fresh and that they learn from any mistakes. They may gradually be asked to do more, or the church may receive a call from another RE coordinator to contribute to a similar lesson at their school.

Helping with RE may seem to be the obvious place to start. However, it can be very rewarding to help with lessons that are not directly religious but allow us to show that being a Christian affects all aspects of our lives, not just the 'holy' bits.

10

Schools visiting churches

When welcoming pupils into church, one vicar asks them, 'Who lives in... (this village)? Who lives in... (this road)?' Then he says, 'This is your church. It belongs to you because you live in this community.'

Every church is a place where people meet to worship God. Whether it is a tiny building like the Celtic chapel at Bradwell-on-Sea in Essex, or a modern architectural wonder like the Metropolitan Cathedral in Liverpool, it is a special place, filled with signs and symbols about the Christian faith.

Children are naturally spiritual beings. They can have a sense of the presence of God from an early age and will respond to the sacred space of a church building. Even the simplest church or chapel can give a feeling of the holiness and presence of God. All churches teach about the Christian faith through their shape, position and enduring presence. Most will teach more through the furnishings, signs and symbols that are found and used in worship.

Many churches already invite their local school to an annual Christmas or leavers' service and would be happy to offer the building as a teaching resource. Other churches and schools may be ready to develop these links.

The benefits to pupils and staff when they visit churches are as follows:

- They encounter Christianity first-hand. This encounter may challenge the stereotyped images found in textbooks or the media.
- They can meet Christians from different traditions in the context of their own worshipping communities.

- They can gain an insight into the wider life of the Christian community and its relevance to today's world. They can see how life issues, such as caring for those who are unwell or elderly, responding to poverty and ethical and environmental matters, are viewed from the Christian perspective.
- It will be a multisensory experience involving hearing, sight, smell, touch and possibly taste. This can help children of all abilities to absorb and retain information. It will also provide an chance for them to explore their own interests and ask questions.
- Such visits are seen to be valuable learning experiences related to Attainment Target 2, 'Learning from Religion', and they help to meet Citizenship requirements for links with local communities.

The benefits to churches when they have visits from schools are the following:

- They build up a relationship between the church and school, which can help the church in its links with the community, both local and worldwide.
- There is an opportunity to raise awareness of the church and its beliefs.
- Churches are made accessible to children and adults who may not be familiar with them.
- The visits allow the children to see that the church is not just a building, but also a living community of believers, giving a 'feel' of Christianity and a sense of the spiritual dimension of life.
- Clergy learn how children perceive the church through the questions and comments that they make.

Getting started

Not many clergy have a captive audience of between 40 and 400, but that is exactly what they get when a class, along with teachers and helpers, visits a church for a lesson, or when the whole school holds a service or event in the building. Opportunities like this have great potential, so they need to be planned well.

Plans to invite schools to visit the church should be discussed with the church council at an early stage. Discussions will cover practicalities such as when the church will be available, and issues about safety and accountability. Any plans should be kept simple, and people who are used to communicating with children should be approached to see if they are willing to welcome the school groups and to support visits.

The congregation needs to be kept informed about the visits to ensure that they are seen as part of the church's ministry in the community.

Some churches have an amazing beauty or visual appeal that can reduce almost anyone to silence, but the decorations and furnishings of any church can create a sense of holiness, whether it is an ancient historical gem or part of a multipurpose modern building. An important first step is for the church council to ask one or two people who know the building and are skilled in teaching or writing to create an information pack about the church. This can best be done by taking a tour of the church and using it as the basis of the information.

Creating an information pack

Teachers need their own starting points when planning work for their pupils. If they are planning a visit, they'll need an overview of the building, explaining its history, architecture and other background points. The overview should be kept brief. A ground plan of the building and a summary of the services and key activities that take place would be helpful.

The following guide may help when creating an information pack or PowerPoint presentation. It would be useful to add any historical or particularly unusual aspects of the building to the guide, similar to the ones in the examples and comments. People may also be able to suggest items for reflection similar to the questions at the end of each section.

Starting outside at the door, walk round the church. Every item in the church can convey a message. Start thinking about how objects such as crosses and pictures tell the Christian story and ask, 'Why is it there? What purpose does it fulfil? What does it say about God?'

The building itself

We learn when the church was built, and something about the people who built it, through the types of stone or brick used and the shapes of the windows, arches and other features. Some churches are cruciform in shape.

Provide information about when the church was built, how it related to the community at the time, and the differences to be seen today. Some ancient churches were once part of the countryside but are now in urban areas. Others were originally part of thriving medieval communities that have now disappeared, leaving the church standing in a field. If the church is part of a multipurpose building, show how it fits in with the other activities that take place. Look at the materials of which the church is built, the shape of the windows and the pillars, if there are any. They will all convey a message.

Example: The chancel of the 14th-century cruciform church in Hellingly, East Sussex bends sharply to the right. This is to illustrate Jesus' head bowed when he died on the cross. The church stands on a circular pre-Christian graveyard. (Norman and medieval graveyards were rectangular.)

A discussion starter might be: 'What can you learn about the people who built this church by looking at the building?'

Furnishings

The font is often by the church door, to symbolise baptism as a person's entry to the Church. This gives a different message from one moved into the centre of the church for a baptism. Baptismal pools (which are often sited at the front of the church) and some fonts are rectangular like a grave, to show how the baptised person dies to sin and rises to new life in Christ. Other fonts are circular to show the perfection and 'oneness' of God. Some are octagonal to symbolise the seven days of creation, plus an eighth day for the resurrection.

The altar or Communion table is always a focal point, either at the far end, so that the pilgrim walks towards it, or central, so that the community gathers around it.

An open Bible placed in the centre of a Communion table or on a large lectern teaches about the importance of the word of God. A Christmas crib, Easter garden, stations of the cross, and prayer board all offer opportunities for teaching.

Some churches have the Bible readings and sermon given from the same place, whether a pulpit or lectern, so making a single focus for the teaching of the word.

Example: The pulpit in the 18th-century Methodist chapel in Walsingham, Norfolk, is raised to the level of the gallery, with a huge Bible commemorating the coronation of Edward VII. This showed the importance of preaching God's word and allowed the preacher to see and be heard by every member of the congregation. Today, the galleries are not used, so the minister preaches from the lectern and uses a microphone so that he can still make eye contact and be heard by everyone.

A discussion starter might be: 'Why are these things here? What do they tell us about God?'

Windows, pictures and carvings

The presence of pictures, icons and statues varies according to the tradition of the church. Orthodox churches show countless saints and angels on the walls and ceiling, to symbolise that heaven and earth are joined through worship of God. The Western church is more restrained in this respect, but some churches may have statues or pictures of Jesus with his mother Mary.

Stained-glass windows and murals taught the Bible to people who could not read. Now that we have the Internet, there is a new emphasis on the visual rather than the written word.

Most buildings will have a cross and other symbols connected with Jesus and his followers on the walls, on banners or embroidered on hassocks. For example, St Peter is often depicted with crossed keys to remind us of Jesus' response to his act of faith: 'I will give you the keys to the kingdom of heaven' (Matthew 16:19). A shamrock is the symbol of St Patrick and tells the story of his teaching on the Trinity: 'Three in one, and one in three'.

Example: A carving by Thomas Huxley-Jones on the south-eastern corner of the south transept of Chelmsford Cathedral shows a modern St Peter wearing fisherman's boots and sou'wester, and carrying a 'Yale' style key.

A discussion starter might be: 'Who are in the windows and murals? What stories do they tell?'

Colour

Medieval churches were covered with colourful murals depicting Bible stories, some in graphic detail. Most of them were destroyed during Cromwell's Commonwealth, to be replaced by whitewashed walls. In recent years, churches of all traditions have come to value the use of colour to aid worship and express the glory of God.

Most Anglican and Roman Catholic churches use 'liturgical' colours on the altar frontal, lectern, pulpit and vestments. Other churches make similar use of colours.

- White or gold are used for Christmas, Easter, feasts such as Candlemas (2 February) and All Saints (1 November), and for baptism.
- Purple is a sign of penitence or sorrow, so it is used in Advent and Lent and for funerals.
- Red is used at Pentecost, on days connected with the cross (such as Palm Sunday and Good Friday) and when remembering martyrs.
- Green is used for all the other seasons of the year, sometimes known as 'ordinary time'.

Example: A modern Baptist church in East London has an octagonal worship area. The wall at the front is covered with hangings to depict the major events in the Christian year: red with flames for Pentecost, dark blue with a cave and stones for Lent, and so on.

A discussion starter might be: 'Why do you think these particular colours have come to be used on those occasions?'

Light

Even the dullest of churches is improved by good lighting. A few carefully placed spotlights can focus on the main features of the church or hidden gems at very little cost.

A candle reminds us that Jesus described himself as the light for the world (John 8:12). Lighting a candle is increasingly being used as an aid to prayer, as well as to express an innate longing for God that is beyond words. Candles show that a church is a place of prayer, which is used by people at all times.

Example: Many churches light a huge Easter (or Paschal) candle, showing a cross, the Greek letters A (alpha) and Ω (omega), and the year. This is a sign of the risen Christ, the beginning and the end, the first and the last—yesterday, today and for ever. It is often placed by the font and the newly baptised person is given a candle lit from it.

A discussion starter might be: 'Why might some people find that lighting a candle helps them to pray?'

Music

Music can express worship more strongly than words. Its beauty gives a glimpse of the glory of God and singing together evokes a sense of corporate belonging.

Most churches use organs to provide music. Others use pianos, guitars and instrumental groups. Some music that we sing is 1000 years old, but in the same service we may sing music that was composed only last week. A huge amount of music for worship has been composed during the last 50 years in a wide variety of styles, and contemporary worship songs have become familiar to many congregations.

Example: Some churches have choirs who wear robes and sit in choir stalls in the chancel, even in modern churches. This reminds us of the monastic tradition. Other choirs sit at the back of the church or in a gallery in order to support the congregation's singing.

A discussion starter might be: 'What instruments and music are used in this church? What message do they send about the way that the congregation worships?'

Other subjects

Is there anything special associated with the church? Maybe there is a memorial standing or plants growing in the churchyard. Gravestones and church records provide an enormous amount of history about people, how long they lived, the number of children they had, and the names that were popular at particular times.

Church buildings can provide practical teaching in several other subjects besides RE, Citizenship and history—for example, art, English, mathematics, music and science. Teachers may not realise that a General from the Crimean War is buried in the churchyard, or that it is a haunt for butterflies. They may not know that the physics of sound can be demonstrated on a pipe organ, or that there is a magnificent view of the town and its meandering river from the top of the tower.

One church created an information pack that included a reflective trail around the church. The building was spacious so the trail allowed plenty of time for the children to explore it. They could go anywhere—see, hear, smell and touch anything. Activities included dressing in the vestments and playing the organ. The information pack included a 'passport' for each child, to be stamped after visiting particular parts of the church. Tasks included studying a particularly evocative stained-glass window and jotting down words to express their feelings about it. After they had completed the trail, there was time for questions. All the teaching and information was very basic, as most of the children had never been in a church before. Some children and teachers knew nothing about the Christian faith. The visit ended with a short prayer and a time of silence so that the children could enjoy the quiet and sense of holiness in the building.

Planning school visits to churches

When the information pack has been made, the church could invite all the local head teachers to breakfast to introduce the church building as a teaching resource. The church can 'set out its stall' by saying what it has to offer and give each person a pack or memory stick. Subjects should be kept broad.

If a school wants to arrange to make a visit, the church will need to know from them:

- The subject of the visit and how it fits with the class's present work.
- The parts of the building, furnishings or objects that need to be especially featured in the session.
- The size and composition of the group, including age, ability range, special needs (including disabilities) and the religious background when relevant.
- Practical arrangements:

  - ❖ Key contact names
  - ❖ Timing and length of visit
  - ❖ Mode of travel
  - ❖ Cost or donation if appropriate

The school will need the following information from the church:

- Contact details of the person who will be present for the visit.
- Maximum and optimum number of children that you can accommodate.
- A copy of the church's own risk assessment if it is required to have one, along with copies of any relevant health and safety and child protection policies.[1]
- Whether there are facilities for parking, toilets and disabled access.
- Whether there is space to leave property or do written work.

Members of staff could be offered a guided tour of the building and the opportunity to ask any questions before the day.

Guidance for clergy and members of the congregation involved in visits

If helpers are working directly with pupils, they should try to avoid simply talking at them and getting them to fill in worksheets. Children will need space to explore their feelings about the church. This may include times of silence, opportunities to focus on a particular object, and encouragement to jot down words to describe the atmosphere and personal feelings.

Children will often want to talk to the person who is there to welcome them or to help generally. It is important to:

- Use language appropriate for the age of the children.
- Keep in mind that some of them will not have been in a church before.
- Expect the children to chatter to each other as they work.
- Predict some of their questions and think through possible answers.
- Help the children to enjoy their visit so that they will have gained good feelings about the church.

- Speak to the teacher or teaching assistant if a child needs help or there is a behavioural issue, rather than dealing with it independently.

It is also important to remember that children will learn more about being a Christian from the way members of the church behave than from the best of lessons in the most beautiful building.

Best practice

The church should be open, well lit and warm, with someone present to welcome the group and show them where facilities are. This person needs to be aware of the focus of the visit and be able to communicate effectively with the children's age group and their particular aptitudes.

If helpers are talking to the children, they must avoid making assumptions about their beliefs.

The Christian story needs to be presented clearly, including the use of Jesus' name. Teachers use RE as a means to teach about people and beliefs. Christian belief is reflected in the shape of the building, its furnishings, its art and its music, all of which are there to facilitate the building's primary purpose of worshipping God.

Some children will be entering a church building for the first time, and it may be the only time they will ever come. An empty building smelling of damp, with bare seats and pointed windows, can seem frightening to some children, and even adults can feel ill at ease. On the other hand, a warm church with music playing quietly gives a feeling of welcome and helps children to relax. It is usually quite easy to have a few spotlights on the altar, pulpit, font or baptistery, and to display any pictures or icons to show which parts of the church are important. A prayer board or candles show that the church is a place of prayer.

The children will need at least five minutes to explore the

building and enjoy its atmosphere before starting the session. This is part of feeling a sense of the presence of God. Occasionally, a child will refuse to enter the church. This is usually because they have seen 'Gothic style' buildings in scary films or have been told stories of spooks inhabiting the crypt. It is best if the child is allowed to sit outside with a teaching assistant to provide reassurance, and go in only if or when the time is right.

Helpers, especially priests or ministers, should be prepared for pupils to ask questions of them. 'Do you live in the church?' is a common question from young children. It is helpful to explain a little about how the church is there to celebrate the important events in people's lives. For example, it welcomes children and adults through baptism, conducts weddings, and also holds a service called a funeral, to remember before God a person who has died. Phrases such as 'You should believe…' must be avoided in favour of 'I believe…' or 'As Christians, we believe…'

The visit can be finished with a prayer or short act of worship. If it is a Church school or the children are accustomed to Christian worship, the person concluding the visit can pray in the way that he or she would when leading worship in school. If that person does not visit the school regularly, or if it is a multi-faith group, it is advisable to ask the teacher beforehand whether prayer would be appropriate. The conclusion to the visit could be related to the theme and include a prayer for the school and the children's families.

Follow-up

It is important to ask for feedback[2] and to encourage the school to be honest with their comments, so that the church can best serve their future needs. The school may be willing to provide some examples of the children's work on the visit, for you to display in church or copy for the church website or magazine.

If a school has produced some teaching materials to use in the church, they may also be willing to provide copies that could be used with other schools. Most teachers are happy to share work, but the name of the school and authorship must be clearly acknowledged on the materials.

Most cathedrals and some shrines have education officers and offer a variety of programmes for children of all ages. A visit to such a place will be a bigger event than a visit to a local church, but it could form part of a day out, with study of the surrounding area and other ancient buildings at the same time.

A final thought

One requirement of all RE syllabuses nationally is that children have the opportunity to visit and explore places of worship. Inviting children to visit local churches enables congregations to open their doors creatively to the schools in their area, so that children can discover more about what Christians believe and what it means to be a Christian today.

11

Clubs and the extended school day

Scott came running out of school waving a piece of paper. 'It's in the holidays. Can I go?' His dad read the flier. A local church was running a holiday club, 'Razzamatazz Robots', in the school. It was a programme of games and other activities with a Christian input: 'Book now to avoid disappointment!'

Having built up a good relationship with the school, there may eventually be a time when the church will want to hold children's activities there as part of its work in the community.

The simplest way for a church to run a club for children is by holding a single event or a short holiday club. The work is concentrated on a couple of hours or a few days and is not designed to be a regular activity. Basic planning is the same for either activity, but the programme and outcomes will be very different. Whatever kind of activity is run, this is an ideal way for a school to provide hospitality to a local church. The offer may be just permission to hire the premises and distribute fliers, but it could also mean staff and volunteers being actively involved.

Single events

There is an infinite variety of one-off events that could be offered for groups of children, with different aims and outcomes. It could be a morning during half-term when a group of children meets to play games and do some art and craft in preparation for a special church service. It could be a 'drop-in day' before Christmas, where children can play while their parents are shopping. It could be a hall packed with children from all the churches in the locality for a day-school of singing or drama. It could be a five-a-side football match against another church or a uniformed organisation on the school playing field. The possibilities are endless.

Some churches, especially in rural areas, have very few children and poor facilities. The churches of a district could combine to hold a fun day, a festival or an activity day for the whole family in a local school.

Since 2001, children from Devon churches, with the help of adults, have met, rehearsed and performed a nativity play from scratch in an afternoon. For the best part of 90 minutes, they have learned songs, practised dances and even made a heavenly host of paper angels. The main characters are chosen and costumes are adjusted to fit them.

Then comes a well-earned breather. Everyone falls on cakes, biscuits and drinks, and then the children take their starting positions for the performance to an audience of parents, friends and people from the children's churches. The musicians give the singers their cue and the well-loved story unfolds of Mary and Joseph's journey to Bethlehem and the events that followed. Animals dance in the stable, a camel train weaves its way around the building, angels sway in the sky, and Christmas has come again.

None of this could happen without a well-organised group behind the scenes, but it is exciting and encouraging to produce and perform a play with music from scratch in a few hours. In addition, the new songs and actions can be taken home to be performed in the children's own churches.[1]

Holiday clubs

Holiday clubs tend to be geared towards children who rarely attend a church, but they are usually open to anyone aged between five and eleven years. They aim to reach children in the locality with the Christian story but they also provide a valuable service within the community. Many families cannot afford to go away for a holiday, so a club or play scheme is an excellent way of providing safe and imaginative play during the Easter or summer holidays. Most children will enjoy a structured time with their friends, whether their parents are at home or at work.

Clubs can last for between three mornings and five days. Published programmes consist of a number of activities and games based on a theme or story with a Christian message.[2]

Midweek clubs

Starting a midweek club of any kind is a major undertaking. A holiday club will last for a few days, and then it is over. A midweek club of any kind will run every week during school term-time, and some may operate more often. This is an enormous commitment.

If the church sees a need for a club or thinks that people have a skill or interest that could be of use, ideas need to be researched and discussed in detail. Questions to ask include:

• Why might this particular midweek club be needed?
• What will be its aims?
• What age group and number of children is it intended to serve?
• Will the school be able to provide the facilities?

The answers to the above questions will give the basic framework. Then the organisation and required resources will need to be considered, including funding. This planning will take some time but needs to be worked out before a proposal can be put forward to the church council or the school.

Resourcing and sustainability

Who will help run the club? Are there people at church or other friends who have the time and skills? How can the church ensure that the club is successful?

There will need to be at least one adult to every eight children if the activity involves child care with varied games and activities. If it is an educational club such as a choir or a photographic club, it will need fewer adults, but there must always be at least two responsible people present. It is important to have a list of reserves who can be called upon at times of emergency, illness or other absence.

Planning needs to be done well in advance, with at least half a term's material prepared for the programme. Other resources, especially funding and personnel, should be identified at least a year ahead. It is best to start slowly with a small project that can be sustained. If the leader has inadequate help, there is a shortage of basic equipment or funds have to be raised to pay the bills, the result will be anxiety and frustration. It is important for the church to start where it is and work within its numbers, facilities and budget.

The chart overleaf gives some idea of the need for thorough planning.

Preliminary research		Shared vision		Adequate resources		Planned first steps		Success
Preliminary research	+	Shared vision	+	Adequate resources	+	Planned first steps	=	Success
		Shared vision	+	Adequate resources	+	Planned first steps	=	Not always appropriate
Preliminary research	+			Adequate resources	+	Planned first steps	=	Fast start but lacks support
Preliminary research	+	Shared vision	+			Planned first steps	=	Anxiety and frustration
Preliminary research	+	Shared vision	+	Adequate resources	+		=	Haphazard, so collapses

Ownership

Will the club be a church project that is part of its service to the community, or will it be a club that is led by a church member?

Both options will need the prayerful support of the church, but there is a difference between a club that is organised and run in the name of the church, and a club that is led by (for example) a parent or a governor who happens to worship at the church. The clergy and church council will have legal responsibility for the former. They will not have the same responsibility if an individual does the work, but it is advisable to involve them in all planning and to remember that the school will judge the church by the work and behaviour of its members.

Funding

Will the school provide the premises and equipment? Will it pay for stationery, food and other materials? If the club is a church project, what sort of budget will the church offer? Might it be possible to secure funds from local councils or charities?

No club can run on air! Even the simplest group will need stationery, refreshments or equipment. Schools are accountable for every penny, so you cannot assume that they will provide help. Work out a budget and take it to your church council. There are numerous other ways of getting funds—for example:

- Local authorities will give grants to clubs if they fulfil certain criteria.
- In rural areas, the parish council, district council and regional countryside agency often give grants for holiday clubs. They sometimes support ongoing projects.
- *Every Child Matters* includes the Children's Fund. Its aims include encouraging better school attendance and educational performance.

- Charities provide a vast source of money and advice. Those to consider include:

  ❖ Children's charities
  ❖ Educational charities
  ❖ Local church charities
  ❖ The Church Urban Fund
  ❖ The Prince's Trust

Accountability

To whom will the club leaders be answerable financially and for the day-to-day running of the club?[3] If the club is taking place on school premises, the organisers will be principally accountable to the head teacher and governors of the school, as the club is there at their invitation. If the club is a church project, it is the legal responsibility of the clergy and church council, so the organisers are also accountable to them. If the club receives outside funding from the local authority or a charity, the organisers are also accountable to that body.

This is not as complicated as it seems. The school will give advice about the organisation and how to report matters like incidents, accidents or a problem with the premises. It will also advise over any matters concerning the children. It is important to keep written records and accounts and report regularly to the church council. Fund providers will probably require an annual report.

Types of midweek clubs

Midweek clubs fall into five main groups:

- Christian clubs in the lunch hour or after school.
- Clubs designed for children with particular interests or skills.

- Uniformed organisations.
- Clubs that are part of a church's outreach programme but held in school.
- Clubs that provide child care, usually combined with activities.

Christian clubs

Leading or helping with a club as part of the school day is a way in which a local church can serve a school. A club held during the lunch hour or immediately after school can offer a specifically Christian programme and involve both pupils and staff.

Aims can include:

- Building relationships and providing pastoral support.
- Giving pupils an opportunity to learn about Christianity.
- Providing nurture and companionship for children who are already Christians.

Of the three aims above, building relationships with the children is most vital and will take time. It will include providing a listening ear and support, as many children will value the opportunity to talk to someone away from the classroom or their home.

The other two aims are not incompatible, but it can be challenging to provide input for children who hardly know the name of God at the same time as nurturing those who are already part of a church family. It is best to try to have activities that are inclusive, rather than relying, for example, on biblical knowledge that only a few children will have. Worship that gives a sense of the presence of God, music, interactive teaching and general discussion can all play their part. It is important to keep everything simple if the club meets in the lunch hour, as time will be limited.[4]

■ A leader of a lunch-time club in a private school described it as 'sharing God's story with those who have never heard it and discipling those who have. It is about making those 40 minutes the best in the child's life that week... Being church, providing pastoral care especially at exam time and family stress moments. We hope that the children and staff are catching what Christianity is, as well as being taught God's story.' ■

EXTRACT FROM DISCUSSION ON 'WHAT'S THE POINT OF LUNCH-TIME CLUBS?'
CHILDREN MATTER WEBSITE, JUNE 2008

A club held immediately after school could involve parents and other siblings. It could be a simple act of worship or a larger event such as Messy Church.[5]

Clubs based on interests and skills

Interests and hobbies can be as diverse as cooking, crafts, drama and war games, but this sort of club can be on any subject where a group of children and some enthusiastic adults share a common interest. Interests could include:

- Art and craft
- Drama and film
- Games
- Languages
- Music
- Sports

Such activities need not be the church's initiative: a teacher may welcome a basketball coach, a second adult for the photography club or a pianist for the choir. Reliability and a degree of expertise and experience are vital. The number of churches that have suitable people will be small but, if there is someone with a skill to offer, it would be well worth exploring whether they could provide an activity in school to the benefit of everyone.

Uniformed organisations

Sometimes uniformed organisations meet in a school. As a meeting place, this has enormous advantages over the average village hall in that the furniture and equipment are designed for children, the building should be clean and warm, and it is a familiar place to some of the members. The advantages to a church are even greater. If the group is sponsored, in that it is formally part of the church's activities or has close links with a church, there will be opportunities for a crossover. Children at the school may join the group and thereby make a link with the church. The church may be able to develop a relationship with the school using the uniformed group as a starting point.

Uniformed organisations have their own structures and training, so they will provide all the information needed.

Church-led activities held in a school

Church-led groups might include after-school clubs, which are run as part of the government initiative Extended Schools (see p. 121), but an imaginative development in some schools has involved church-run activities for toddlers and pre-school children in the school.

Finding suitable premises for pre-school groups can be a problem, but it may be possible for a church to use a classroom sometimes, if the timetable permits it. If the school hall were available, there could be an occasional drop-in session for parents and toddlers before the end of the school day. It would be relatively easy to set out chairs and create a safe area with soft mats and toys, and perhaps a couple of people from the church could help out with the group. Sessions could be finished with a circle time, to include a story or a song and maybe a prayer.

Pre-schools are big players in the provision of education for all children under five years of age. Consult your local education office to find if there is a need for such a group. If there is, carry out careful research and seek as much advice as possible before further planning takes place. If there is a shortage of pre-school places in the local area, the local authority will give you every support. Leaders will have to be trained and the group will have to be registered and regularly inspected by Ofsted. The work is rewarding, however, and a church-led group can provide the first way for many young children and their parents and carers to hear the Christian story.

Again, one of the main advantages of holding an under-5s group in a school is that the premises and equipment are designed for children. If the plan is to run a permanent group by renting a classroom, some adaptations may be necessary but it will be better than a multipurpose church room or hall. A pre-school on the premises could provide a valuable halfway house to 'big school' and may encourage parents and carers to consider sending their children to that school rather than another. Finally, there will be the potential to provide links between the school and the church.

It may, however, be possible to hire a classroom on a short-term basis only. If the school's roll grows, the group may have to vacate at a term's notice. That is a risk worth taking, but it is advisable to have some sort of contingency plan ready.

St Mary's primary school had had a falling roll for some years. After discussion with the new head teacher, it was decided to offer one of the empty classrooms to the church for its pre-school group. This proved highly successful. The pre-school children sometimes joined the Reception class children for collective worship and special events. They also used the hall and playground when they were available. Many of the children moved up into the main school and, with this development and gradually improving standards, the roll grew to the point where the classroom was needed again. The pre-school had to move into the church hall, but it continued to maintain links with the school. ▪

Child care

Child care includes breakfast, after-school and homework clubs. These groups are almost all run by commercial companies as part of the Extended Schools provision, but churches that already have successful midweek clubs for children might want to consider whether they can develop their services by forming a partnership with the local school. This could be a wonderful opportunity for involvement within a larger structure.

In some schools, there are waiting lists for breakfast and after-school clubs. If the church hall is available and of a reasonable standard, helpers might be able to hold a similar club on church premises, with a 'walking bus' to take the children to or from school.

Extended Schools

The Extended Schools programme is part of the government's *Every Child Matters* agenda as well as being the most recent stage in its policy of providing 'wraparound' care for children and young people at the beginning and end of the school day. It is, in part, a response to the increasing need for flexible child care. It also makes use of school facilities for longer hours so that children can enjoy learning support to help them with their education, and a variety of extra activities and hobbies. Some of the activities are also open to adults.

By 2010, all schools will be providing a full range of services either on their own or in clusters. Some services will be free but others, like child care, will incur a charge.

The services offered come under five main headings:

- Child care
- Activities for children
- Parenting and family support
- Easy access to specialist help
- Community access

As well as breakfast, homework and after-school clubs, there could be opportunities for churches to run or help with special interest clubs or a uniformed organisation. Schools may be especially interested in anyone who offers a creative, well-planned activity for children who are from disadvantaged backgrounds or are underachieving in school. This sort of work is a wonderful example of Christian service, but it is important to remember that such children may have many other needs and a considerable amount of skill and patience will be required.

Helping children is often a result of helping parents. Such help can go far beyond the traditional parenting classes: it includes encouraging parents to help their children to read or just to feel at ease in school.

A failing school in an area of extreme deprivation invited parents of the Reception class children to come into school on Friday mornings to read to their children. This activity became quite popular but the majority of the children still had nobody to read to them, as some parents were nervous about coming into a classroom. Eventually a grandparent who was an experienced children's leader offered to read to a group with their parents. This had a calming effect on the class so it attracted several parents who gradually gained confidence to start to read to their own children.

A final thought

If you think that there is a need that could be filled, sound out your vicar or minister, then research the idea thoroughly. It may seem that the need is obvious but plans to address it may be in hand, so it is essential to find out whether a new club or group could be duplicating a service, with a loss to both groups. Plans to start a group should always be taken to the church council before the school is contacted.

It is important to be flexible and think creatively about the church's assets. Also, there may be possibilities for collaboration. For example, a local school may be needing help from volunteers, or two churches could combine to run a joint project.

All ongoing clubs require commitment and organisation. At their best, they present enormous opportunities for a local church to be involved in enriching children's lives and supporting their parents. They may also provide Christian teaching and values to young people who will not find them elsewhere.

*

— 12 —

Voluntary help

My contact with schools started when I volunteered to help.
Since then, both my career and ministry have grown. I am now
employed as a part-time teaching assistant and plan and deliver
RE lessons, which are filed with the RE coordinator. I still work
as a volunteer by taking seasonal programmes to other schools.

TEACHING ASSISTANT, MALMESBURY, WILTSHIRE

There are far more ways that a church can establish a link with
a school than by leading worship, helping with RE or organising
visits to the church. Each church is a community of Christians
from all walks of life who live out their faith by serving, befriending,
supporting and engaging with people wherever they find themselves
—including the local school, where helpers can have an amazing
impact. Even the smallest congregation can form some kind of link
with a school, provided there is goodwill on both sides.

People volunteer to help in school for all sorts of reasons. It is
usually because they enjoy being with children and have experience
of teaching or leading a children's club. Sometimes, it is a way of
finding out more about what it is like to work in a school. There
are also people, however, who are lonely, need to be wanted or
feel that they have to help with anything that the church is doing.
Their needs are real, and a caring church community should help to
address them, but it may be that these are not appropriate people
to be working with children or vulnerable adults.

Rather than asking for volunteers, it is often more effective to
approach people who may have the qualities and time to help in
school. The following criteria are a useful way of assessing suitable
people.[1]

- Previous experience of looking after or working with children.
- Ability to provide warm and consistent care.
- Willingness to respect the background and culture of all children in their care.
- Commitment to treating all children as individuals and with equal concern.
- Reasonable physical health, mental stability, integrity and flexibility.

As we have already seen, anyone who is working regularly with children will be required to apply for a Criminal Records Bureau enhanced disclosure.[2]

The following list gives some idea of the many ways in which a congregation can own and support its local school. You may be able to think of others. Every school has its own needs, every congregation has its own skills, and it is just a case of matching them up.

Everyone can:

- Pray for the school—when they walk or drive past it or as part of their personal prayer time. The school can be included in the intercessions in church at the beginning and end of term, at exam times and on special occasions—for example, when the appointment of a new head teacher is taking place.
- Attend school fundraising events such as fêtes, or a school service. The staff will appreciate the support and interest and helpers will probably recognise some of the children.
- Encourage a young person who enjoys being with children to consider a career in teaching or other schools work.
- Include the school in discussions on education or evangelism at the church council.
- Save supermarket vouchers if the school is collecting them.

The church council can:

- Invite the school to display artwork, provide music in church or take part in a service.
- Offer the use of the church for school plays, concerts and other events.
- Ensure that work with schools is reported and noted at meetings.
- Ask the head teacher if some children could contribute to the church magazine.
- Welcome school groups to the church building and churchyard for RE and other lessons.

Someone who is housebound can:

- Pray for the school. They can be given copies of the school magazine or newsletter to keep them involved.
- Help with a task such as sewing a costume for the school play. It is too easy to deskill people who are frail, and most people love to feel that they can be useful.

Someone with a little time to spare regularly can:

- Assist in the classroom or with reading groups. This can be voluntary help, but might also lead to training and employment as a teaching assistant.
- Join a parents' group and be involved with fundraising, pastoral support or social events.
- Become a school governor.[3]
- Help in the office, with lunch-time supervision or at a second-hand uniform stall.
- Offer a skill such as playing the guitar, coaching football or helping with drama or other clubs.

Someone who is used to working with children can:

- Help with breakfast or after-school care.
- Hold a fun morning, holiday or midweek club on school premises.
- Run a 'Christian Union' type of club during the lunch hour.

Someone who is able to offer occasional help can:

- Help with school events, sports day, a class outing or Christmas parties.
- Welcome and provide information to children when they visit the church.

Clergy or trained lay people can:

- Lead or help with acts of worship and special services.
- Provide ongoing pastoral support to staff and pupils.
- Teach or help with RE lessons.
- Listen to and advise staff or parents who have difficulties. Some schools have a parents' support group for this purpose.

The following story shows how even the smallest church can build a creative relationship with a school if just a couple of people have imagination and enthusiasm.[4]

Two people from a team of six small parishes in Devon were so inspired by a diocesan training day on building relationships with schools that they invited the diocesan children's adviser to speak to their team council, to 'enthuse the troops'. She spent an evening in a packed village hall discussing ways of engaging with children beyond Sunday. Six weeks later, the two enthusiasts had approached the four schools in their benefice to invite them to join in a big harvest celebration, which would include a focus on the needs of children who live in areas of famine. Three of the schools joined in. Each school prepared a 20-minute musical or dramatic presentation on a different aspect of harvest, coordinated by the churches. One looked at the wonder of creation, another celebrated harvest bounty, and the third considered the inequalities of food and poverty across the world. Each school included prayers that the children had written. The event was a high-quality experience for the children, which met many of the requirements of the National Curriculum as well as being an act of worship that drew the schools and churches together. The two organisers, one of whom was a parish children's leader, visited each school afterwards with a gift of biscuits for the teachers. ▪

Knowing the boundaries

Most teachers are committed and highly professional people, but a few may be tempted to use a helper as a way of getting some time to do marking or other jobs. Helpers should never take a class without a teacher present and should always refer to a member of staff before making decisions. It is important to attend meetings whenever possible and insist on being briefed. Helpers should always support the school's policies and decisions, even if they do not personally agree with them. Above all, they must value each child, even if he or she is driving them crazy!

Being welcomed into a school puts a volunteer in a position of trust. Inappropriate behaviour, a badly prepared act of worship, careless talk or unreliability can undermine years of patient work between a church and school. It is an abuse of trust if contact with the children is used to play on their emotions, to start an inappropriate relationship or to invite them to a particular church. Head teachers who are wary about inviting Christians into the school have usually had a bad experience at some time and are not willing to risk exposing their pupils and staff to another one.

A final thought

A Christian presence in school may lead to questions and opportunities for discussion with members of staff and parents. Working with children in school is a great privilege and responsibility as well as presenting enormous opportunities.

13

School governors

Being a governor is a good way to get involved with a school. There is a shortage of suitable people and it gives an automatic entrée and a relationship as well as some .influence... When I said that I had experience as a school governor, they bit my hand off!

NEW VICAR AFTER VISITING THE LOCAL PRIMARY SCHOOL

Every school is managed by a governing body. School governors are the largest single group of volunteers in the country and play a significant part in the education of every school-aged child. Their work is unpaid and sometimes undervalued and unrecognised. On the other hand, many school governors have served their schools for decades and thereby made an enormous contribution to the community as well as thousands of young lives.

Owing to the legal responsibility they carry, governors have to be aged 18 years or over on the day of election or appointment, but there are arrangements whereby young people of less than 18 years can be associate members of a governing body. Governors are also expected to sign a declaration of interests and may be required to undergo a CRB enhanced clearance.[1]

What sort of people are governors?

Governors come from all walks of life. No special qualifications are needed; nor do governors have to have a prior link with the school. They just need the will to make a difference to children's education. Not everyone has the inclination or ability to work directly with children, but some people have an interest in the field of education and have experience and expertise that could be put to use as a governor.

Governing bodies welcome people from the local community who understand what it is like to live there with a young family. They need people with experience of building, the law, employment issues, local government and, perhaps most of all, finance. Finance is discussed at every meeting, so a governing body is indeed fortunate if it has a member who understands and can speak with authority about budgets and balance sheets.

■ Someone who had recently retired from management of a cleaning business volunteered to be on the board of governors of a primary school in a deprived area. He soon found that the head teacher was having difficulty with an unsatisfactory caretaker, so he offered to manage the caretaker. Standards in the school's maintenance improved markedly, with a positive effect on the school's morale, and a good working relationship developed between caretaker and governor. A few years later, the governor supervised the repainting of the school building. ■

Being a governor

Some people think that being a governor would be an interesting way of serving their local school and believe that they have a skill to offer, but still wonder if they are the right sort of person. What would be expected of them? Apart from attending a couple of meetings each term and reading through the papers before it, governors need to gain a working knowledge of how a school is run. Anyone who is a parent, has worked in a school or is a member of a church that already has contacts with a local school will probably know quite a lot already.

Governors need to be sympathetic to the ethos of the school—

the way it values children and helps them to achieve; the way it meets the needs of children with learning or behavioural difficulties and children who are from minority communities or suffer from deprivation. As Christians, we should value all children, but the way this valuing is expressed will differ from school to school. Similarly, not all Church schools will express their Christian beliefs in the same way. Some will have stronger links with the local church or give higher priority to worship than others. Some will have a large proportion of children from other faiths and none. A Christian governor can be highly influential but he or she is there to serve the school, not to use it for personal ends, however laudable they may be.

■ 'We are here to serve the school, not the other way round.' ■

SHEILA MARSHALL-TAYLOR, CHAIR OF GOVERNORS AT CHRIST CHURCH SCHOOL, CHORLEYWOOD, HERTFORDSHIRE

Being a governor goes beyond simply attending meetings of the governing body. Staff and pupils will notice and appreciate it if a governor goes to school events or visits the school while it is in session: it is enough just to be seen to be there. Governors will also learn a lot by going to an act of worship or sports day, or just by walking around the building and chatting to the staff and pupils.

■ 'Are you a teacher, Miss?' asked a very small boy.

'No, I am a governor,' I replied.

'What's that?'

'Well, I am a friend of the school and I try to help your teachers to make it a happy place.'

'That's cool!' he commented. Then he ran off. ■

THE AUTHOR BEING 'INTERVIEWED' ON HER FIRST VISIT AS A NEW GOVERNOR

Membership of the governing body

The governing body is made up of a mixture of elected and appointed representatives of groups in the community, staff and parents. The governing body appoints some individuals itself. The present composition in any small primary school might be:

- Two elected parent governors.
- Two elected staff representatives.
- Local authority appointees.
- Members of the local community and up to two sponsor governors, appointed by the governing body.

NB: The head teacher does not have to be a governor, although naturally he or she will attend meetings. The two staff representatives are usually one teacher and one representative of the non-teaching staff.

Church schools have a slightly different composition, with 'foundation governors'—that is, members who are appointed by the parish church and the diocesan Board of Education. In an Aided school, the foundation governors will form the majority on the governing body. In a Controlled school, they will be in the minority.

Although there is no formal church representation on the governing body of non-Church schools, many invite a local vicar or minister to be a governor as a representative of the local community.

Anyone who is interested in being a governor might like to consider being on the governing body of a community school rather than automatically supporting a Church school. They may be the only Christian voice in that community, so they can ask questions and help to ensure that there is appropriate support for subjects such as RE and worship, as well as having an influence on policies concerning pastoral matters, special needs and sex education.

What do governors do?

The governing body is responsible for seeing that the school is run so that each child has as good an education as possible. Its duties include:

- Setting strategic direction, policies and objectives.
- Approving the school budget.
- Reviewing progress against the school's budget and objectives.
- Appointing, challenging and supporting the head teacher.

Governing bodies are divided into committees that report to the main governing body about specific issues, such as the school's curriculum, premises or finances. Anyone who becomes a governor will probably be asked to serve on a committee where they have some expertise or a particular interest.

The time spent being a governor (beyond the meetings) can depend on a person's own level of interest but the DCSF (Department for Children, Schools and Families) suggests that 6–8 hours a month in term time is probably a realistic level of involvement. Some employers recognise the vital work done by school governors and will allow them time to attend school events or meetings during the school day. Governors are also entitled to claim travel expenses.

This may all appear daunting, but it is worth remembering that a governor does not have to be an expert on every subject discussed and is not individually responsible for any decisions and their consequences. Both head teachers and governors have expert advice and training to hand from the local education office and, in the case of Church schools, from the diocesan education department. This advice will include information and briefing about any educational changes or issues, so that governors are kept up to date. Local authorities offer governors training and advice on a regular basis.

There are, however, a few qualities that will be helpful for any governor. First is an eye for detail and an ability to read and digest information correctly. Next comes a willingness to ask questions, whether on a small point that needs clarification or on the difficult issues that take courage to address but upon which a lot may depend. It also helps if governors are computer-literate, as most of the information and training is published online, but this is not vital. Lastly, a governor needs to be 'on the ball' about the standards and expectations of the school. A useful source of such information is Ofsted's website www.raiseonline.org, which provides interactive analysis of school and pupil performance data.

Relationships between governors and head teacher

An experienced chairman of governors described the relationship between the head teacher and governing body as being rather like the relationship between the monarch and his or her government. The governing body is there to inform, advise and, when occasion demands it, to warn.

The head teacher will look to the governors (and especially the chairman) for interest in everything that is going on, for support and advice in decision-making, and for participation in tasks such as being the third person present at a tricky meeting with a member of staff or a parent. One term that we often hear, as a description of the governor, is 'critical friend'. This is the ideal relationship, but it is far easier to talk about than to build in reality. It requires mutual respect and trust, and a professional attitude which recognises that any criticism will be made out of interest in the other person's well-being and the good of the school community. It takes time and experience to develop.

In a report on training by Anne Holt and Peter Downes, *Working Together: Great Expectations—Getting the Head/Governor Relationship Right*, ten governor expectations of head teachers were listed.

1. Accept that accountability is necessary and that governors have a right to ask questions.
2. Accept that governors are part of the school. Make the governing body part of a learning organisation and facilitate training and development opportunities.
3. Accept that although governors are voluntary they have a professional job to do and are not amateurs.
4. Share with us your vision and your goals.
5. Put things that matter on to the agenda.
6. Make your report to the governing body meaningful and give us the information we need to do our job effectively.
7. Encourage us to check things out for ourselves.
8. Seek our permission and accept our protection for those decisions.
9. Ensure that the governors receive proper servicing.
10. Remember that the education of the young people comes first for us as well as you.

Pastoral care

Christian governors have the potential to become 'big picture' people, modelling Christ in the way they value everyone regardless of age or position. A child who is not coping at school for some reason is as important as a head teacher with an infirm spouse. Parent and community governors are especially well placed to provide support because they probably meet children and staff outside school and may be friends and neighbours to some of them.

Sending a note of appreciation or providing the encouragement of a phone call or conversation can also have an incalculable effect at the right moment. A contribution like this is not token support but an essential act of love—recognising and respecting the intrinsic worth of every human being, wherever they are in the school community.

Lynn was a voluntary helper in the local primary school. She became well known to the other parents and was elected as a parent governor. Staff valued her reliability and common sense. Pupils knew her as someone they could trust, who would listen and laugh with them. A teacher was bullying one ten-year-old girl. The youngster felt isolated so started refusing to go to school. Her mother was worried but did not know the reason. Lynn approached the mother and asked if the child would like someone to 'help her to get through the door' in the morning. On their walk along the road each day, the little girl started to talk about her unhappiness. Lynn gave her the courage to tell her mother and the head teacher so that the difficulty could be addressed.

Lynn was also a bellringer at the local church. She established a team of pupils to ring the bells for the school's carol service. Each year they spent an afternoon practising with her and then went out to tea. Several of them became ringers at the Sunday services.

What to do next

If you are interested in becoming a school governor, try to find out more informally from another governor or a head teacher. Then discuss the possibilities with your vicar or minister. He or she will probably have been a school governor at some time so could be a useful sounding board.

For the next step, you could contact a local school to ask if it needs a new governor. The local authority will also be able to help you to find a school or advise on opportunities to become a governor. If you want to serve in a Church school, contact the Diocesan Director of Education (DDE) at the diocesan office. The DDE will know which schools in the locality need governors and can give advice.

If you are a parent of children in the school, a first step could be to talk to the present parent-governors and decide whether to stand at the next election for parent-governors.

A final thought

Anyone who becomes a school governor will find that the work is demanding but always interesting and potentially highly satisfying. They will also find that they have gained a new 'family' in the school community. This shows itself in a number of ways, not least by finding that a number of small children will wave shyly, point the governor out to their parents, and even run up in the street saying, 'You come to my school!'

14

Chaplaincy roles in school

Most of the pastoral care is through informal conversations as they arise, but senior staff members also refer students to me. I try to be available to listen at any time but will make an appointment if I cannot see someone immediately. For a while I shared my office with a local policewoman. This was really useful—sometimes I would join her to stroll around the playground and on the truancy patrol in the local cafés and shops. We had a policy of talking through the 'cause and effect' of situations rather than handing out proscriptive punishment. I find that I often act as a sounding board for staff over personal needs, but also when there is frustration over issues connected with their work.

CHAPLAIN OF AN ANGLICAN COMPREHENSIVE SCHOOL IN NORTH LONDON

The majority of employed chaplains are in secondary schools but there are a few in primary schools. The 'chaplains' described in this chapter are, for the most part, clergy doing the work as part of their ministry in a local church. Some employed children's or youth workers have chaplaincy as part of their job description and a few lay people take on chaplaincy work in a voluntary capacity. A tiny number are members of a school's staff.

Every school is a distinctive community within a local context. Legislation, SATs and league tables, combined with expectations from parents and the media, tend to make head teachers and staff inward-looking. It is for the prospective chaplain to take the first step to demonstrate the possibilities in his or her contribution to the school's daily life.

Most chaplains are involved in the school's worship. They may lead collective worship, or work with staff and students to develop creative and significant worship that is at the centre of the school's life. They can also contribute to a school's spiritual life by leading voluntary worship for small groups. This might include a prayer group for staff and parents, a Eucharist before or after school, a leavers' service, or simply ending the first day for the new Reception intake with a short prayer.

Other ways in which chaplains have given help include:

- Being playground supervisors
- Coaching football or netball
- Directing or writing a play
- Hearing children read
- Helping with sewing or craft
- Playing a musical instrument
- Photographing special events

Pastoral care

Pastoral care is based on forming good relationships. The school office is a good place to start, because members of the administrative staff meet everyone from the parents to the postman. They know every child and member of staff, as well as the daily workings of the school. They are a valuable source of information and practical help.

It takes time to build relationships with the teaching staff and it is important to learn the school's set-up, its strengths and its weaknesses. Gradually sharing ideas with teachers, asking for feedback after an act of worship or lesson, and generally 'chewing the cud' together can achieve this. A school chaplain will learn from the expertise of the teachers and, in return, teachers will begin to have confidence in the chaplain and gradually recognise that he or she is at hand to listen.

A 1980s housing development includes a triangle of shops, with Asda, the church and a primary school at its three corners. The priest-in-charge has gradually made herself known to the school, leads some collective worship and has been called in to provide support at times of difficulty. The school has recently started to use the church for harvest and Easter and the priest is now invited for coffee in the staff room. She is also chaplain to the staff and customers at Asda and often does her shopping at about 4pm, 'loitering with intent' so that she meets families from the school.

Although teachers may travel a distance to work, non-teaching staff usually live locally and may have long-term connections with the school. Sometimes chaplains are asked to take funerals for relatives of local staff, students or people who have had links with the school. For example, when a young man was killed in a motorcycle accident, his parents returned to the school and church of his childhood for the funeral.

Chaplains who are on the board of governors can often mediate in difficult situations or advise on appropriate action. Parents, as well as staff, often approach the chaplains with questions about the school as well as personal matters concerning finance, relationships or illness. One chaplain describes his relationship with his school as being akin to that of the 'father of a community'. He is not just a teacher or chair of governors, although he appointed all the staff and teaches for a day each week. Members of the staff recognise the distinction between his various roles and respect them. They know he is alongside them to celebrate as well as comfort. Parents and staff approach him when they have problems and also enquire about having children baptised or their home blessed.

Chaplains can also run 'chill-out' groups during the lunch hour for older children. This allows time for discussion and general chat as well as providing company and friendship. Being a Christian in school can be isolating so it is helpful to have a place and time for Christian pupils to meet. The chaplain is slightly detached, so children can relax and talk freely with someone who is not involved with their work or classroom issues.

Lay chaplaincy

Lay chaplains are few in number and most of them have specific roles. An affluent church or a group of churches may employ a children's worker, whose brief might include contact with local schools. This contact may involve leading worship, helping with PSHE, running a lunch-time or after-school club and some pastoral work. Organisations like Church Army and Scripture Union also employ schools' workers.[1]

Lay chaplains are either trained leaders in their own churches, with a background in education, or teachers who have the role as part of their pastoral work. For example, a school governor who is a retired teacher and lay preacher is chaplain to a primary school in the Midlands. A Head of RE who was also a pastoral assistant became the chaplain at a secondary school.

Support for chaplains

The School Chaplains' Conference is part of the Bloxham Project, which exists to support the spiritual dimension in education. It offers pastoral and intellectual support for chaplains, as well as training and professional development opportunities.[2] Diocesan CME and schools' officers will also offer specialised advice and training.

Lay people can also support the chaplain's ministry. Their role is important because they are 'ordinary Christians' who have a variety of jobs and different interests and skills. Having members of the congregation to welcome classes to the church building and at school events is a powerful way of showing that the local church is more than just a building.

Transformation

The following case studies tell how two schools were transformed into flourishing Christian communities. The work involved a lot of people but, in both cases, the chaplain played a crucial role in the development.

Developing the spiritual life of a junior school

A parish near Bristol consisted of five churches and four denominations. It had two Church schools. Ann, the team vicar, was asked to focus on the two schools, one an infant and nursery school and the other a junior school. The schools were very different and few children moved from one to the other. The infant school was a flourishing community with a stable staff and a good reputation. The head teacher was a committed Christian and the school's Christian ethos permeated through everything it did. The worship and RE were strongly integrated. Themes included seasons and the liturgical year, with background teaching in class. Ann was immediately able to contribute to the established pattern.

The junior school was a Church school but provided a less evident Christian environment. Ann started to lead worship and help with RE lessons. She became the vice-chair of governors, so she was involved in staff appointments, the head teacher's appraisal and the curriculum. When the head teacher left and her deputy was appointed, Ann gave her ongoing pastoral support as a listening ear and sounding board.

Under the leadership of the new head teacher, the school developed a more Christian ethos. Year 2 children at the infant school began to move automatically to the junior school, instead of going elsewhere. The head teacher realised that they needed to look at the school's spiritual development and worship holistically, and worked with Ann to develop more creative worship. Prayer corners were formed and used at particular times. The creative worship included a prayer walk in Holy Week.

Local practice hindered the school from developing eucharistic worship but Ann started having a Holy Communion service for the staff of both schools at the beginning of each year. It was kept informal, with displays as a focus for prayer to involve people who were not used to worship. Almost everyone attended the services, which were well received and valued.

When Ann moved on, she was not replaced. The new deputy head teacher, who had come to faith during her time at the school, took on much of Ann's chaplaincy role as well as coordinating the RE and worship.

From Special Measures to success

An outer London primary school in a deprived multicultural area was in Special Measures and facing closure. A failing local secondary school had become a successful Church of England school so, as a last resort, the borough went to the Diocesan Board of Education for help. There was a strong will for the school to succeed. Agencies, the local authority and the DBE worked together. Although the pupils came from diverse religious backgrounds, there was very little opposition to the school becoming a Church school. New governors and a new head teacher were appointed and Clive, the local vicar, who was already a governor, became the chair of the new governing body.

Five years later, the school is flourishing. A nursery school was started as part of a strategy to increase intake to the main school. It has 70 children aged from six months, with its own manager. There is an Extended School with a Sure Start centre on the site. This also has its own management but the manager is a governor and meets regularly with the head teacher.

The admissions policy is based on residence in the parish. This prevented problems when the school was changing status, and has worked well. Twenty-three languages are spoken in the school. Many of the children are members of Pentecostal churches, and the intake also includes Sikhs, Muslims and Hindus. Their leaders and other Christian clergy are welcome guests in the school. Clive and the head teacher set up a Christian ethics group to explore the nature of a Christian school. Members of staff are expected to participate in collective worship and uphold the Christian values of the school. Clive is present when the head teacher meets parents to deal with behavioural problems. They see him as a visible reminder of the ethos of the school and the behaviour expected by its members.

Some of the children have joined uniformed organisations, and there is a confirmation preparation group in Year 6. Clive is frequently in school and often calls in to the nursery to play. The nursery teachers are young and include several single mothers, who need companionship and a sounding board. Clive has an annual 'pastoral conversation' with each member of staff. The meetings are confidential but he feeds back any general needs to the head teacher. Everyone finds the meetings very helpful. They boosted confidence at a time when the school was struggling and morale was low. At Christmas, Clive serves the entire staff with drinks and mince pies in the vicarage.

A final thought

There is no typical job description for a chaplain. 'Pastor', 'critical friend', 'encourager' and 'listening ear' are some of the terms that chaplains use to describe their role. The work is demanding and needs skills and training as well as time, but one of the few common characteristics is that every person working in a chaplaincy role in school regards it as a vital part of their ministry and speaks of it with enthusiasm.

Children's and schools' workers

As part of the PCC's strategy to develop the work with children and young people, it was decided, after prayer and discussion, to appoint an experienced worker to minister to children and families. The time seemed right to do this when our curate left, so that a stronger focus could be given on working with local schools as well as building up the work within the church.

BRIAN FORTNUM, ST MARK'S, BROADWATER DOWN

Professional children's and schools' workers are like chaplains in that they make a valuable contribution to a school as part of their work, while not being employed by the school. Some of them are children's or youth workers who have contact with local schools as part of their job. Others are employed by a Christian organisation or a group of churches to work specifically in schools. In both cases the work can vary from occasional visits to working in a particular school for one or more days each week.

Being a children's worker

Many children's workers are gap-year students, recent graduates or people taking a break for a couple of years while exploring a vocation or change of career. Others are former teachers or people who have considerable experience of working with children in a voluntary capacity. The post is usually on a fixed contract for three or five years. Salaries are varied and may include accommodation. Sometimes the job is treated as work experience or a practical placement for a student with an honorarium and accommodation provided.

It is sometimes assumed that children's work is identical to youth work but with smaller people. This is far from being the case. A child aged six is very different from one aged 16. Moreover, children of primary school age are dependent on the goodwill of their parents to be involved in activities outside the school day or travel beyond the immediate locality, so any work with children automatically involves young families.

Training in children's work varies. The increasing number of accredited courses is a response to the growing demand for professional qualifications commensurate with the responsibilities of the work. Even if a children's worker is employed on a short-term basis, NVQs in subjects like child development, and specific training like the ecumenical course, *CORE Skills*,[1] should be a minimum requirement for anyone doing this sort of work.

Working in school

Children's workers may be involved in leading acts of worship, helping with RE or PSHE lessons or running clubs in the lunch hour or after school. They may be part of a support group for parents experiencing difficulties. They may also be a sympathetic but detached listener for a child who wants to talk about issues at school or at home. They will have interests and skills that can shape the work and help them to be of service to the school. In short, the job is whatever the worker and the head teacher decide to make of it.

■ St Dunstan's, Cranbrook, is a town centre parish with a secondary and two primary schools. In 2005, it appointed Louise, a former teacher, as a children's worker while she studied for a diploma in children's evangelism and nurture at Cliff College. It gave her practical experience and she was allowed twelve hours each week for study. In the primary schools, Louise led collective worship and started lunch-time and after-school clubs. She also provided curriculum support through taking classes to visit the church. Other work ranged from providing pastoral care and teaching when a pupil died to being interviewed as part of an Ofsted inspection.

Most children's workers find that the best way into a school is through leading collective worship. Many schools struggle to provide worship of a high standard and appreciate the input and help that can be given by trained and experienced leaders from churches. Leading collective worship makes children's workers visible and can be the start of building up relationships and becoming part of school life.

If this relationship is going to be effective, however, it is important that the workers are kept involved in the daily life of the school. This should include receiving information on matters like serious illness or death within children's families. At one school, a children's worker started an act of worship by asking what children had thought about that morning. A boy replied, 'My mother.' Fortunately, the worker just said, 'That's nice': she had not been told that the boy's mother had just died.

Children's workers can also make themselves visible as part of the school's life by being involved with events at school and in the wider community.

Schools' workers

Specialist schools' workers have a slightly different role. Most of them serve a number of schools and may be employed by evangelistic Christian organisations such as Spinnaker Trust, Church Army, or the London City Mission. They provide a Christian presence in schools and are involved with worship, RE, PSHE and pastoral care. Some of the work may include organising and leading a group such as a Christian Union or an after-school club. These groups will include children who are not involved with a church in any other way.

A large church will sometimes fund its own schools' worker but it is becoming increasingly common for a group of churches, such as a local Churches Together team, to set up a trust to employ a schools' worker. Imaginative approaches like this can occasionally receive funding from local charities, as they are seen to be providing community cohesion as well as service.

Scripture Union is involved in ministry in schools by working with students, staff and parents. This includes taking lessons, leading collective worship and running lunch-time and after-school clubs. Currently there is a national team of schools ministry specialists based in various locations. They have three distinct roles:

- To help churches make the most of opportunities to link with their local schools. This is achieved by building relationships, running training events, putting churches in contact with schools, helping to establish lunch-time and after-school clubs and directing people to relevant resources.
- To coordinate networks of those who go into schools as part of their job, such as youth workers, children's workers and church leaders, and to equip volunteers to provide appropriate support to schools.
- To support schools in their task of delivering RE and addressing issues related to spirituality, PSHE and Citizenship.

GEOFF BROWN, SU SCHOOLS' WORKER, TYNESIDE

Finding help

Most major denominations have children's and youth advisers who can help with providing support and in-service training, as well as giving guidance about job descriptions, employment and similar issues. It is a good idea to invite a children's adviser or member of a children's committee to be part of the interview panel when appointing a schools' worker. Several diocesan bishops in the Church of England commission their employed children's and youth workers and give them permission to preach at church services.

Scripture Union runs a scheme that enables groups of churches to form a charitable trust to employ a schools' worker. It offers help and advice at every stage, from registering as a charity to raising funds and conducting interviews, as well as managing a worker on a daily basis. It also provides information on employment legislation and training opportunities for both the trust and the worker.

AMAZE is an association of Christian children's and youth workers that promotes professionalism and best practice in the work. The AMAZE manual is a complete guide, which includes support and information on employment issues.

Amicus (part of UNITE) is a trade union with a section for clergy and church workers. Benefits include support, advice, insurance and legal representation on all matters.

The Schools Ministry Network is a voluntary group of Christian organisations and individuals working in schools. As well as promoting high standards and sharing of resources, it encourages churches to be involved in their local schools.

More information about organisations supporting work in schools will be found in Appendix 1.

A final thought .

Whatever their brief, church-based children's and schools' workers are part of the church's mission among children and their families. Their work is of enormous value but it can be very isolating, especially if a worker is young or living in an unfamiliar area. Clear line management, a structured week (with a day off) and an opportunity to worship occasionally at a church not connected with the work should form part of any contract. A personal mentor, spiritual director or support group that is not connected with the particular church is vital in providing guidance and friendship as well as being a sounding board over work-related matters or decisions.

Making the school visible to the church

The school has become an integral part of the church's life. It has a high profile at all the main church celebrations. The children take part in the opening procession with their school banner. A pupil reads one of the Bible readings, and the choir sings an anthem. The school always provides an entertainment, such as dancing, at the church fête. Their artwork is regularly displayed in church and they contribute stories, poems and drawings to the church magazine.

ST GEORGE'S C OF E PRIMARY SCHOOL, BICKLEY

Many churches have a lively relationship with their local school. Some Church schools are seen to be an integral part of the church, either because the school building is used regularly for services or because the school itself is a Christian community, with prayer and sometimes the Eucharist at the heart of all that it is and does. Other churches may have an equally strong but different relationship with a school, whether it is a Church school or not. A minister or priest will lead collective worship regularly and occasionally help with RE lessons. Members of the congregation are on the board of governors and may be involved in other ways. The children use the church building for RE and history lessons, and may have an annual service there. The church holds a summer holiday club in the school, and so on. Yet, even if these events are reported to the church, the congregation may not realise the importance of such a relationship or even know that it exists at all.

A larger number of schools have a good relationship with the church. Some pupils and their families attend the church, one or two of the congregation may visit or work at the school, clergy may occasionally be involved, and children may visit the church building.

Even so, the relationship can be almost invisible to the congregation.

So how can the school become visible to the church and, through that, make the church visible to the wider community? Most of the following suggestions take just a little work. Some are more time-consuming but in each case the rewards far outweigh the effort involved.

Art and craft

Artwork displayed in school is seen only by the children and staff, and has to be taken down after a short time, either at the end of term or to be replaced with another display. Sometimes the children take their work home, but many families find it difficult to display it in a way that shows that they value it. The church could offer to display some of the children's work for a further period or during the holidays. If you decide to do this, identify suitable display areas before approaching the school, and agree how long the work will be displayed and who will remove it. Ask the teachers to label each piece of artwork with the name of the school, the child and his or her class, and tell the children and their parents that the work is on display.

Churches may also consider asking if a class can provide artwork for a special church occasion. For example, paintings about creation or the seasons would be suitable for harvest time, and displays for Christmas and Easter could be taken into the church at the end of term. One primary school provided a series of paintings that were displayed around the church and used as prayer stations during Lent.

If the school is used for church services, it may be possible for the wall behind the table or altar to be decorated with a suitable backdrop. For example, pupils invited everyone in one school to draw an outline of their hand on a piece of white paper to make into the wings of a huge angel.

The possibilities are endless but each one depends on the situation, people, time and talents at hand. Whatever is done, it allows the school to contribute to the beauty of the church as well as giving the church a chance to enable parents, the congregation and wider community to learn something about the school and enjoy the artistic achievements of children in the community.

Drama

Some primary schools find that their hall is too small for their needs. It may be difficult for the whole school to meet together for collective worship and, if the school has an annual show or play, there is the additional problem of finding space for an audience of families and friends. One solution may be to move popular productions to the church. This has the double advantage of allowing a larger audience to see the show and enabling children and families alike to enter their local church in a non-threatening situation.

Although the church may not seem to be the obvious building to use, especially if it is ancient and possibly cold, it is worth talking through the possibilities with the head teacher. Most churches have a raised area that makes a natural stage. This can be extended with staging blocks or benches if necessary. There will be at least two entrances, one from the vestry at the front, the other from the back. Some churches have side aisles, and pillars can be good places for hiding a prompter or for allowing short times 'off stage'. Pews can become houses or even a mountain range. The pulpit can be a boat, the top floor of a house, a tomb or a home for angels.

High voices can get lost in a large building, but children can be taught to speak clearly and slowly. Some churches have their own sound system, which could also be used with practice. Lighting may present a problem, but most lighting effects can be achieved with simple spots and hired floods. Wooden pews are not the most comfortable seating, but add 'Bring your own cushion' to the publicity and the problem is solved at a stroke.

Even if the school does have good facilities, the head teacher may still consider the invitation to give a repeat performance of the nativity play or another production in a local church. A lot of work goes into drama, so teachers and children alike may welcome the opportunity to perform to a different audience.

■ Christopher is a former music teacher as well as being an Anglican priest. As well as leading worship and being a governor at his local primary school, he helps with the music there. After four years of planning with the staff, he directed a school production of *Joseph and the Amazing Technicolor Dreamcoat*. The church was used for the final performance because it was bigger than the school hall, and was packed out with members of the congregation as well as parents and friends. ■

If the school's drama is based on a Bible story or includes a reflection used in collective worship, it might be possible to include it in a Sunday service. Some pupils may not be able to come to church on Sunday because of other commitments, so it is best to have a few children to hand who can be slotted in at short notice, and also to use groups rather than individuals. A child could read an extra prayer to fill a gap—and many an Epiphany procession has had only two wise men!

Music

A school concert can also be held in church, with the same advantages and challenges. Singing and instrumental music inevitably sound better in a resonant church building than in a school hall, once pupils have got used to projecting their voices in the larger space and enjoying the sound.

If the school has a choir or pupils who enjoy singing, they could be invited to sing at a special service or with the church's own choir. If pupils are joining with the church choir, rehearsal time is needed, but everyone should gain from the experience of having all ages singing together. If the school has a strong musical tradition, some instrumentalists may be willing to play at a service. This is a big job as it involves transporting instruments, writing out parts and rehearsal on site. However, if it can be done, few experiences are more rewarding for the music teacher and youngsters, and families will usually come to support their children.

A simpler option is for a child or a few children to play before the service, at a time of reflection after the Bible reading or sermon, or during the offertory.

Taking part in services

As well as through art, drama and music, staff and children can represent their school on occasions such as Education Sunday or special festivals. If a new vicar or minister is appointed, it is important that the school is represented at the induction or service of welcome, as it is part of the community where he or she will be serving. Members of the school, both adults and children, can take an active part in any service by reading a Bible passage or leading the prayers. On some occasions the head teacher could be invited to give a talk.

Education Sunday

Education Sunday takes place on the ninth Sunday before Easter, so it will fall at the end of January or beginning of February. It is a time for reflecting on the church's role in educating children and adults in the Christian faith, giving thanks and praying for those who teach and those who learn. Education means something far broader than just going to school: it is a lifelong experience in which the local church has a vital role. Toddler groups and pre-schools are the biggest growth point in many churches and, at the other end of the scale, the Church has colleges and other places of higher education as well as numerous training courses. Most local churches provide Christian nurture for children and many offer study groups of some kind. That said, most people automatically link education with school, so Education Sunday is a golden opportunity for the school to raise its profile as well as thanking God for the year's blessings and praying for the months to come.[1]

Staff and children could be involved by:

- Welcoming the congregation by handing out books or service sheets.
- Reading a Bible passage. The passage could be read dramatically, mimed or acted in place of the sermon.
- Leading the prayers. Each child could have a short petition on a card and stand in a line, with a hand-held microphone being passed along. Another option is for a small group to take turns at the lectern or in the pulpit.
- Speaking about Christian education. The head teacher could be invited to contribute in this way.
- Displaying a PowerPoint presentation about the school at the back of the church after the service.
- Leading the singing or singing a special item.
- Playing music before or after the service.
- Displaying artwork in church or illustrating the service sheet.
- Presenting representatives of the school to be commissioned during or at the end of the service.

Other services

Harvest thanksgiving is another occasion when the children could have an input, as well as bringing food for those less fortunate than themselves. Their contribution could be linked with work in school on environmental issues, farming, the seasons, how plants grow and a charity connected with the developing world, according to the age of the children.

Mothering Sunday can be a tricky day, given the commercial pressures and the associated difficulties for some children who do not live with their mothers or even know them, but it is an ancient practice to give flowers to mothers and to thank God for those who care for us. This could be extended to giving thanks for everyone who cares for us, whether they are mothers or not, as well as focusing on Mary the mother of Jesus and, if appropriate, the image of the 'mother church' caring for us all.

At Christmas, the school could be involved in a festival of carols by providing music and some of the readers. This is always a well-attended service where non-church parents can feel relaxed. Christingle services and crib services are other possibilities.

The school could be represented at services involving a new or departing vicar or minister, or the church could participate in saying farewell to a longstanding member of staff or greeting a new head teacher. The school could also be invited to civic services. If there were a death among the staff or pupils, it would be appropriate for staff and children to go to the funeral, if they wished. It is important for children to have an opportunity to say 'goodbye' to a friend or someone who has been important in their lives. Most children cope better with the service than is expected of them.

If the school has eucharistic worship, it could transfer a service to the church, which would give a very different feeling for pupils used to the school environment.

A final thought

Whatever the opportunities, it is important for the church to recognise that extra work will be required on the part of staff and pupils. It will be necessary to give help and support by exploring only what is possible and not making overly heavy demands on an already crowded curriculum. On the other hand, it will give a wonderful opportunity for the members of the church and the school to meet each other and share resources.

Churches using school buildings

For many years, our church used a nearby primary school on Sundays as a base for its thriving children's work. As a child, I assumed that this was the building's sole purpose, because I was educated elsewhere!

CHRIS HUDSON, BARNABAS CHILDREN'S MINISTRY TEAM

For many years, local schools have supplemented their income by hiring their premises to local people and organisations. Not every church owns its own building and some congregations will hire school premises, while others meet in community centres or church buildings of another tradition. In areas where there is a new residential development, a church may decide to hold a second service on Sunday or midweek in the local school, because it is more accessible than the church building. Some ancient church buildings have no facilities so they use the school for the junior church or for coffee afterwards. Most schools are happy to have their premises used in this way, because it increases their income and serves the community in a practical way. Some may positively welcome the opportunity to develop their relationship with a local faith community.

Any decision involving the use of buildings has huge logistical as well as financial implications. Having one's own church building provides a permanent place for prayer, with opportunities for services and meetings every day of the week. Church property can be used whenever it is needed. The costs, however, of owning and maintaining a building that may be used infrequently are often prohibitive, and congregations do not necessarily have the resources to adapt their building for modern use.

A church meeting in a school, or using it for some of its regular services and activities, will find a totally different situation. The burdens of maintenance, furnishing, heating and cleaning are covered by the rent. The premises will be modern, with proper heating and toilets. They may be nearer to where people live and more accessible for people with disabilities and young children. On the other hand, the church will have to find independent storage space and will need to plan in time and organise helpers to set up before and clear away after every service or other event. The church will be a tenant, with other events happening on the same premises, so long-term planning is vital if there is to be wider use than a regular booking on Sunday mornings.

Advantages of having a church based in a school include:

- It demonstrates that the 'church' is the people of God wherever they are, rather than a building where people go to worship him.
- The church is not maintaining a building that may be used on only one day in the week.
- Some people are ill at ease in a traditional church building. Everyone will have been in a school at some time, and it is a familiar and welcoming place for most young families.
- Some schools have car parking space, and it may also be possible to use the playground.
- Schools are usually near to residential areas. Halls are usually set at ground level and are accessible for adults who are frail, have disabilities or are bringing young children.
- Schools are fundamentally child-friendly. Their displays and furniture are designed to stimulate young minds and to fit young bodies.
- Classrooms can be used for group discussion, prayer, one-to-one ministry and youth and children's meetings. The school grounds can be used for social events.
- There is potential for the school and church to work on shared projects.

There are also possible disadvantages of using a school. Here are some examples of the potential difficulties and ways of addressing them:

- Turning a school hall into a church involves planning and ingenuity. Everything from silver to service sheets has to be transported. Furniture and furnishings have to be rearranged. It is not, however, such a time-consuming task as some people envisage. A school might be able to offer some storage space and include setting out chairs as part of the rental agreement.
- Priority for bookings is usually given to school events, so forward planning will be vital. If the music group or choir needs to rehearse before the service, it must arrange for the school to be opened earlier. Midweek clubs have to fit around other activities, so make sure that your particular club is booked well in advance. If a group plans to meet during the school holidays, it will be necessary to check that the building will be clean and heated.
- The furniture in a primary school is usually designed for young children. However, most schools will have a stack of full-sized chairs in or near the hall. If the church wishes to hire the use of a classroom, it is preferable to ask for one used by older pupils. Equally, the staff room or library may be a suitable venue for any situation where elderly people are present.
- Some people may find the displays distracting during services, but this distraction tends to diminish with familiarity. Colourful and pleasant displays may be more conducive to prayer than the plain white walls of many churches, and will serve as a reminder to pray for the school and the subjects that are displayed. Consider using flowers, banners and displays to help to transform the space.

Best practice

Establishing a good system will enable the church to maximise the benefits and minimise the disadvantages of using school premises. Some examples are outlined below.

Respecting the premises and surroundings

The caretaker will be the linchpin in ensuring that the premises are ready for services and meetings, so give priority to establishing a good relationship and showing consideration and appreciation from the outset.

It is vital for everyone to remember that they are guests in someone else's place of work and to treat it appropriately. Few things are more frustrating for a teacher than to have to console children because their work has been damaged or hold back a teaching programme for several weeks because valuable equipment has to be repaired. If anything is damaged, it should be reported immediately and paid for, if a cost is involved.

Classroom layouts are a key part of any teacher's behaviour management system (requiring a lot of planning in September), so furniture and items must be replaced in exactly the way they were found. Teachers know the precise layout of their classroom, and it is a good idea to take a digital photograph or make a clear sketch before moving any furniture, other items or piles of books. If the class whiteboards are used, they should be cleaned afterwards. Board pens should never be used on a Smart board, which is linked to a computer system.

The school's hospitality should never be abused by using rooms that have not been included in the hire agreement, and equipment should not be borrowed without permission. School stationery or the staff's coffee should never be used. This is stealing and, apart from moral considerations, it is bad witness for Christians to be less than scrupulously honest.

Using school equipment

Most churches will want to serve refreshments after the service. All schools will have kettles and urns for heating water. Some will have warming cupboards and trolleys but only a few will have fully equipped kitchens, and the church will probably have to provide its own crockery.

All school halls should have audiovisual equipment and a piano. It may be possible for the church to borrow them, and most schools would rather make them available than have untested electronic equipment used on their premises. Some music departments have valuable electronic instruments. It may be possible to borrow them, once a good relationship is formed and the Head of Music is confident that they will be treated carefully.

Permission should always be obtained before using any of the school's equipment.

Maintaining good relationships

By-laws and local residents' association regulations should always be checked in the early stages of planning to see if there are any restrictions that need to be noted. Special consideration should be given to people who live near the school. Although the local residents will be used to the noise of children playing and leaving school, they will not want to be disturbed on Sunday morning when they are trying to have a lie-in. Cars should be parked considerately and unnecessary noise, including music, should be avoided.

If a church wishes to develop its ministry by using the school more frequently, it should make clear what the activities will be when additional bookings are made. Most schools are happy to cooperate with reasonable requests but the head teacher needs to be advised of any plans before that stage, so that both they and the governors can ask relevant questions or make suggestions.

Worshipping in a school as a new experience

Congregations worship in schools for a variety of reasons. So far, the discussion has been about the practicalities of hiring school premises and the implications for potential churchgoers. An important point to consider is how a congregation steeped in the tradition of worshipping in a dedicated church building will react to worshipping in a school. How will it have a sense of the presence of God and come away renewed to serve him in the community?

Sometimes there will be a sense of excitement and an awareness of new possibilities that have not existed before. Sadly, however, some churches have to move to a school because the church building costs too much to heat in the winter, major repairs are needed, the structure has become dangerous or there has been a fire. There may be a sense of loss and grief in these situations, so leaders need to be sensitive and work hard to make the school building 'church' again for people.

Creating a sense of worship and a sacred space

Just as an atmosphere for worship has to be created in a traditional church building, so it has to be created in a school. A new situation will be accepted in time. The key is evolution, not revolution, and always to give the best experience possible.

Pointers for creating sacred space include:

- Have everything, including plenty of adult-sized chairs, set out in plenty of time.
- Be extra particular about tidiness.
- If the church uses candles, banners or vestments, continue to use them.
- If people are used to being greeted quietly, continue in the same way.
- Play appropriate music as people arrive.
- Consider making a few innovations that capitalise on the new space. For example, consider having the service 'in the round' or utilising different areas. Elderly people and young families might appreciate having tables for their books and other belongings.

It is important to remember that it is God who makes a place holy and to allow the sense of his presence to take over. It may come through the powerful singing or an inspiring sermon. It may be in the silence left at the end of the prayers, or the space left to reflect on a Bible reading. For many people, it will be when they receive Holy Communion. Even the most traditional worshippers may find themselves surprised by the sense of the presence of God at these moments. Any good act of worship can be inspiring, and everyday spaces become sacred as God makes himself known. He is present among the plastic chairs, the tea urn in the corner and the table normally used for school dinners, as much as he was during Jesus' earthly ministry on a beach or by a Samaritan well.

A Victorian church in Lambeth was in such a poor state of repair that plans were made to sell the prime site and build a small modern church on a smaller piece of land. By the time the church was demolished, however, building costs had soared and the congregation became homeless. For several years they worshipped in the local school hall. Every Friday evening it was laid out as 'church'. A trestle table became the altar, placed in front of seasonal backdrops painted by the school children. The organist became a pianist and the choir sat on PE benches. On special occasions the school recorder and percussion groups helped to accompany the hymns. The staff room doubled as a vestry and a place for making coffee. A tall cupboard provided storage. The small congregation thrived as they worked together and relations with the school strengthened. Babies were baptised there. The room was packed for the memorial service for a past vicar. Somehow, the school hall where the children played games and ate their lunch had become a holy place.

Using the school as a second building

Even if a church has its own building, it may still decide to hire a school for weekly or occasional events. Churches without halls may use the school regularly for youth and children's activities such as midweek clubs, uniformed organisations or an event such as Messy Church, and occasionally for large events such as the annual general meeting, a holiday club or the harvest supper. Some churches will occasionally hold a service in a school as part of making their worship available to the wider community. All of these events have potential for strengthening the relationship between the church and the school.

A rural medieval church with no facilities was separated from most of the houses and its school by a busy dual carriageway. Links between the church and school were fragile and few of the children attended the church. The new rector started to build a relationship with the school by leading some worship and then establishing half-termly services. Parents had normally only attended the school nativity play and Mothering Sunday assembly but they were invited to attend the half-termly services, too. The new emphasis on worship and strengthening of links between church and school had the effect of encouraging several families to become involved in the church. The junior church flourished and started to meet in the school, where it had plenty of space and good facilities.

A final thought

The possibilities of using a school vary from running an occasional meeting there to almost sharing the premises. Some churches base all their gatherings in a local school, and use people's homes for administration and small meetings. The potential depends on the individual situations and needs but, with prayer, careful planning and goodwill, much can be achieved to the benefit of all concerned.

*

— Afterword —

Barnabas in schools

In 1999, BRF (Bible Reading Fellowship) began its 'Barnabas in schools' programme. This has now grown and is implemented by a national team of full-time and freelance professionals, who together have worked in over 700 schools across the UK.

From the outset, the Barnabas children's ministry team was concerned to work professionally and creatively with primary schools by adding value to their RE curriculum and helping busy teachers to deliver reflective, enjoyable acts of collective worship and interactive, thought-provoking lessons. This meant listening to what teachers needed and putting together workshops on themes that contributed positively to the QCA guidelines for good RE practice, while also taking into account current initiatives in RE and other areas of the curriculum. Keeping up-to-date continues to be a priority for the Barnabas children's ministry team as it has responded to new developments such as Citizenship education, Values programmes and the SEAL curriculum.

The first Barnabas RE Days were trialled in local primary schools in the south of England. Building on feedback from these days, the ministry team developed a number of themes, which are explored using Bible stories, drama and interactive storytelling. New members of the team have added further creative arts to the repertoire, including mime, music and dance.

A Barnabas RE Day aims to fulfil a number of key objectives for teachers. It is an opportunity to give RE a higher profile within the school by offering a special focus day in which all year groups participate, after a keynote assembly that introduces the topic. The day gives learners an alternative medium through which to explore Christian beliefs and the meaning of Christian festivals, majoring on active learning that helps children to 'step into stories' and learn from RE, not just about it. RE Days are also a way in which teachers can develop new skills and gain confidence in the teaching of RE as they observe new approaches demonstrated in the workshops. Finally, and most important, a *Barnabas* RE Day aims to be fun, while at the same time promoting thinking skills and creativity in line with good practice throughout the rest of the curriculum.

The range of RE Day topics is growing and new ones are constantly being developed. At the time of writing, the themes include:

- Whose world? (Looking at our responsibilities towards creation)
- Who am I? (Looking at issues of identity and self-worth)
- Who is my neighbour? (Looking at compassion for others as well as community cohesion)
- What's so special about the Bible? (Majoring on the Bible as the Christian's special book)
- It's not fair! (Looking at issues of justice, both locally and globally)
- Christian festivals (such as Harvest, Advent and Christmas, Lent and Easter)

In each workshop the aim is to include a mixture of active learning through play, participative learning through drama and other creative arts, and reflective learning through different styles of storytelling. In all the sessions, Bible stories are key elements of the workshop, and there are follow-up activities for teachers to use with children on the website, www.barnabasinschools.org.uk.

The *Barnabas* RE Day team comprises trained teachers and people who have extensive experience of working in schools. This has proved a really important strength as it has enabled team members to empathise with teachers as well as to be trusted by them. The team develops new ideas together, combining its creative talents in a way that has earned respect from RE advisers and other professional organisations. It is not uncommon for other schools' workers, local clergy and members of congregations who go into schools to join the team on one of their RE Days, to learn from them by working alongside the team in the classroom.

Over the years, the *Barnabas* children's ministry team has also developed further dimensions to its work, including in-service training for teachers (INSET), looking at issues related to delivering Christian RE creatively; special RE Days hosted at central venues for a number of schools together on major themes (such as festivals) or for special occasions such as Year 6 leavers' days; and contributions to teachers' conferences, school exhibitions and local authority training days nationally.

All of the ministry team's work is supported by a wide range of published books for schools, written by teachers and developed from class-room use. In addition, the website www.barnabasinschools. org.uk is regularly refreshed with new ideas and useful links for teachers.

Key to the success of '*Barnabas* in schools' has been its willingness to listen carefully and respond to the needs of teachers as well as the demands of the RE curriculum. As such, it is a partnership that puts into practice the principles explored in this book. Many local churches have sponsored an RE Day in their local primary school and have benefited and been inspired by the expertise and example of the team. This has helped them in their desire to forge positive links between local church and local school.

To find out more about '*Barnabas* in schools', write to:

Barnabas in Schools
Team Administrator
15 The Chambers
Vineyard
Abingdon
OX14 3FE

Alternatively, telephone 01865 319704 or make contact via the web on enquiries@brf.org.uk. Visit www.barnabasinschools.org.uk to find details of all programmes, published resources and ideas for assemblies and lesson outlines.

*

Information and websites

The following list is not exhaustive but will provide further information on most of the subjects mentioned in this book.

Schools and other local education matters

Each maintained school is listed under its local authority, usually a county or a borough. It will be listed in your telephone directory and will have its own website. Schools will be listed on the website under 'Education'.

Church schools

General information about Anglican and Roman Catholic schools will be found via your diocesan office. It will be listed in your telephone directory and denominational handbook and will have its own website. Each diocese has a Director of Education and may also have an RE adviser.

Other denominations will be able to provide information about their work with schools. If you cannot get information locally, contact their national office by phone or via their website.

Training

The Church of England offers training for clergy and some lay people on working with schools. Contact the CME (Continuing Ministerial Education) Officer at your diocesan office for further information. It may also provide training and support for children's and youth workers. Contact the youth or children's adviser as above.

The following websites refer to organisations or government departments mentioned in the book.

4children	www.4children.org.uk
AMAZE	www.amaze.org.uk
Association of Christian Teachers	www.christian-teachers.org.uk
Barnabas in Churches	www.barnabasinchurches.org.uk
Barnabas in Schools	www.barnabasinschools.org.uk
Beat Bullying	www.beatbullying.com
Bloxham Project	www.bloxhamproject.org.uk
BRF	www.brf.org.uk
CARE for Education	www.care.org.uk
Children Matter	http://childrenmatter.ning.com
Church Army	www.churcharmy.org.uk
Collective worship and family service material	www.sermons4kids.com
Criminal Records Bureau (CRB)	www.crb.gov.uk
Data analysis for schools	www.raiseonline.org
Department for Children, Schools and Families	www.dcsf.gov.uk
Education Sunday	www.educationsunday.org
Every Child Matters	www.dcsf.gov.uk/everychildmatters
Independent Safeguarding Authority (ISA)	www.isa-gov.org

Learning Outside the Classroom   www.lotc.org.uk

London City Mission   www.lcm.org.uk

Messy Church   www.messychurch.org.uk

National Society   www.natsoc.org.uk

Office for Standards in Education (Ofsted)   www.ofsted.gov.uk

Open the Book   www.openthebook.net

National Curriculum   www.qcda.gov.uk/13575.aspx

RE Inspired   www.reinspired.org.uk

School governors   www.governornet.co.uk

Schools Ministry Network   www.schoolsministrynetwork.co.uk

Schools work   www.schoolswork.co.uk

Scripture Union   www.scriptureunion.org.uk

Spinnaker Trust   www.spinnakertrust.org.uk

Qualifications and Curriculum Development Agency (QCDA)   www.qcda.gov.uk

UNITE (formerly Amicus)   www.unitetheunion.org

*

Step-by-step through a school Eucharist

The following are general principles that will prove helpful.

- Keep the worship moving while allowing time for silence and reflection.
- Cut out all unnecessary words and optional prayers.
- Use prayers that the children have composed themselves.
- Include movement, music, drama, art and visual aids.
- Remember that it is easier to sing than to speak together.
- Let the children lead all of the service apart from the parts reserved for clergy.
- Never exclude a child from worship or deny him or her a blessing.
- It is best to avoid too much standing and sitting. Consider standing for all prayers and music, and sitting for readings and during the administration of Holy Communion.
- A class Eucharist could be celebrated 'in the round', even with very small children seated around a low table that is used as an altar.

Preparation

- Have the altar table set out with a display to illustrate the theme.
- As the children assemble, sing repetitive songs and rounds.
- Have a procession with a cross, candles and servers, if used in the parish.

Greeting

'Welcome to our school / class Eucharist…

'Today we are thinking about… In our Bible story today we…

'But first we need to remember the times that we have let down God, each other and ourselves.'

Penitential rite

Allow time for quiet reflection. Use simple petitions written by the children, or a 'sorry' song.

The prayer for forgiveness can also be written by the children or be a simple 'May almighty God have mercy on us, forgive us our sins and bring us to everlasting life. Amen.'

On special occasions, the penitential rite could be followed with a simple sung setting of the *Gloria in Excelsis*, such as the 'Peruvian Gloria', Mike Anderson's 'Clap hands Gloria' or a simple version familiar to the children.

Collect

This could be the prayer for the occasion or could be written by the children.

Readings

You may wish to include just the Gospel reading. There are several ways of presenting readings. For example:

- A child could read a version from a children's Bible.
- Some Gospel and a few Old Testament readings lend themselves to being read in parts.

- The reading could be mimed. Mime needs careful timing, with a reader who will pause while the action is completed.
- A short drama based on the reading could be enacted.
- The reading could be concluded with a song to illustrate it or reflect on it.

Prayers

- Have short bidding prayers written and led by the children.
- Have a response for everyone to join in. This could be sung.
- PowerPoint images could be used to illustrate the subjects.
- Some prayers could include actions—for example, the 'compass prayer' in which the children point up to praise God, point down to pray for the world, extend the arm to the right to pray for others, and point inwards to pray for themselves.
- Children could write prayers that are collected in baskets and laid before the altar. NB: Such prayers are personal between the child and God, so they should not be read and must be destroyed afterwards.

Preparation of gifts

Children could present the elements. They could offer examples of work, a Lent project or class activities at the same time. Children who find work difficult or who do not participate in other ways should be included. The time may be used for a dance or a song.

Eucharistic Prayer

The Church of England is currently producing Eucharistic Prayers for use with children. The present *Common Worship* Eucharistic

Prayer H or a variety of prayers from other traditions are commonly used.

For the Memorial Acclamation, a song such as 'Jesus breaking bread, sharing bread: Jesus drinking wine, sharing wine' (*Kum ba yah*), 'He is Lord' or 'Jesus, we adore you' could be used. Everyone should join in the final 'Amen'.

The Lord's Prayer

Use the version familiar to the children, with everyone joining in, perhaps with hands held out. A small group could stand around the altar with hands joined. There are several gestures that are sometimes used to illustrate each line, but these could be made up by the children.

Communion

It is advisable to make Communion as inclusive as possible by accepting communicants from all traditions and offering everyone a blessing. It is quickest if people move forward in two lines and remain standing, then move outward and back to their places. It is important that no child is excluded because of age or a behavioural issue. Exclusion could give a message that this child is beyond the love of God, with possible harm caused in the future. Have instrumental or recorded music, ending with a 'thank you' song.

A final thought

High-quality worship requires work and constant review. It is better to do a little well than to try to do everything suggested in the above outline. A school Eucharist may be very successful but each service has to be carefully prepared so that it is kept fresh and responds to the changing situation. Every summer, the oldest and most experienced year group leaves and is replaced by children who are new to school and probably to worship. At the same time, other children's talents may come to the forefront. This presents both challenges and opportunities, so each service will have a different character from the previous one.

✶

Church visit evaluation form

Evaluation form for schools to complete after a church visit
Name of school
Number and age of children
Aims and learning objectives of the visit
Were the above areas covered in the visit?
What were the most successful parts of the visit?
Were there areas that should have been covered differently or more fully?
Are there any ways that we can make school visits more successful?
How will you follow up your visit in the classroom?
Is there any way that the church can be of further service to your school? Please return this form to .... Thank you.

*

Notes

1. Christian vocation

1. *The Way Ahead: Church of England Schools in the New Millennium* (Archbishops' Council, 2000).
2. There are examples of people doing this through working in school on pages 126–127.

2. Christianity and schools

1. This became the National Society for Promoting Religious Education in about 1930.
2. The National Society founded most Church schools of the period but this is an example of one of the few that were founded by individual clergy or a parish church.
3. The poorest children were eligible for scholarships.
4. Often known as the 'Durham' report.
5. Office for Standards in Education.
6. Now known as Foundation schools.
7. See pages 49 and 55 for further information.

3. Schools as part of God's mission

1. There is more information on attainment targets in Chapters 5 and 9.
2. There is more information about this in Chapter 14.
3. There is more information about churches using schools in Chapter 17.
4. For more information about Messy Church, visit www.messychurch.org.uk
5. For safety reasons they used glow sticks instead of candles.

4. Forming a relationship with a local school

1. Chapter 12 contains useful information and lists of ideas for voluntary help.
2. There is information on this in Chapter 11.
3. See Chapter 5, page 41, for further information.
4. There is more about this in Chapter 16, page 154.
5. For information on Barnabas RE Days, see www.barnabasinschools.org.uk.
6. Stories of volunteers who now deliver RE lessons and lead a prayer group as well as helping in other ways are in Chapter 12.
7. This is described in the Afterword on pages 170–173.

5. Legislation and best practice

1. See Appendix 1.
2. For further information, visit the ISA website: www.isa-gov.org.
3. There is more information on this in Chapter 12.
4. Sir Jim Rose, *Thinking Primary* (QCA, 30 April 2009).
5. There is more information on RE in Chapter 9.
6. There is more information on worship in school in Chapters 6—8.
7. There is detailed information on school visits to churches and the opportunities they provide in Chapter 10.
8. This is discussed in Chapter 10, pages 99–105.
9. Chapter 13 covers the work of governors and parent groups.

6. Collective worship in school

1. There are examples of this in Chapter 8.
2. Now known as a community school.
3. There is more about this in Chapter 9.
4. There is more about this approach in Chapters 14 and 15.

7. School as a praying community

1. See www.natsoc.org.uk.
2. There is more about the pastoral role of clergy in Chapter 14.
3. There is information about liturgical colours in Chapter 10 (p. 102).
4. There is more information on school visits to churches in Chapter 10.

8. The Eucharist in school

1. *Common Worship*, The Archbishops' Council (CHP, 2000).
2. See www.cofe.anglican.org for further information.
3. See Chapter 14, pages 143–144, for Ann Mackenzie's story about the transformation of a school near Bristol.

9. Religious Education, PSHE and Citizenship

1. See the chart in Chapter 5 (p. 49).
2. Making the first contact with a school is described in Chapter 4.
3. Church visits are the subject of Chapter 10.
4. Read through the section on taking part in collective worship in Chapter 6 (pp. 55–64) for advice about presentation and speaking.
5. An example of a primary school's teaching about these services is described in Chapter 8 (p. 81).

10. Schools visiting churches

1. A church that employs more than five people, including clergy and part-time workers, must have a written health and safety policy.
2. There is an evaluation form in Appendix 3.

11. Clubs and the extended school day

1. The original version of this story was published in Margaret Withers, *Mission-Shaped Children* (CHP, 2006).
2. For details of holiday club programmes, see www.barnabasinchurches.org.uk.
3. There is information about the legal obligations of working with children in Chapter 5.
4. For midweek clubs programmes with a Christian theme, see www.barnabasinchurches.org.uk.
5. For more information about Messy Church, see www.messychurch.org.uk.

12. Voluntary help

1. Home Office Guidelines, *Safe from Harm* (HMSO, 1994).
2. See Chapter 5.
3. See Chapter 13.
4. From a report by Rona Orme, first published in *Mission-Shaped Children* by Margaret Withers.

13. School governors

1. See Chapter 5.

14. Chaplaincy roles in school

1. See Chapter 15 for more information.
2. Details of these organisations will be found in Appendix 1.

15. Children's and schools' workers

1. Consultative Group on Ministry among Children, *CORE Skills for Children's Work* (Barnabas, 2006).

16. Making the school visible to the church

1. For further information, see Appendix 1.

Index of subjects

Accountability
    Clubs in school...116
    Collective worship 55
    Governors...136
    Visits to church..98
Art and craft 80, 110, 118, 154–155
Ash Wednesday 81
Audiovisual equipment... 165
Bible (see Collective worship, Religious Education)
Bible references
    Deuteronomy 6:20–21, 23–24 8–9
    Numbers 6:24 72
    1 Samuel 3:1–20 16
    Psalm 78:3–7 8
    Isaiah 2:2–3...83
    Matthew 3:13–17 81
    Matthew 5:13 16
    Matthew 5:16...17
    Matthew 6:21, 33 11
    Matthew 16:19...101
    John 8:12 103
    Acts 1:8..25–26
    Acts 9:8–19...16
Cathedrals
    Education officers 72, 75, 109
    Schools' festivals..75, 77
Chaplaincy (see also Religious Education, Collective worship)
    Funerals..141
    Governor 141
    Lay..142

Listening ear 145
Mediator 141
Pastoral care 140–142
Support for ....'........... 142–143
Transformation: case studies 143–145
Worship leading 139–140
Charities
Funding from 116, 150
Speakers from 62
Supporting 82
Child protection (see Health and safety, Legislation)
Children's activities
After-school clubs 27, 32, 119, 121, 122, 127, 142,
149, 150
Breakfast clubs 32, 121, 122, 127
Christian Union 127, 150
Church clubs in school 119–121
Extended Schools (see Government initiatives)
Funding for 115–116
Holiday clubs 26, 27, 110, 111–112, 115, 168
Interests and hobbies 118–119, 121
Lunch-time clubs 142, 149, 150
Midweek clubs 112, 116–121, 127, 163, 138
Ownership 115
Planning clubs 113–114
Pre-schools 119–121, 158
Resourcing 113
Single events 110–111
Uniformed organisations 111, 117, 119, 122, 168
Children's workers
Employment of 151
Schools' workers 62, 142, 149–150, 152
Support for 151

Training as a.. 148, 173–174
Unions and associations.. 151
Work involved 148–149
Christian education 18, 20–21, 158
Christian organisations
Barnabas in Schools 170–172
BRF 170, 174
Church Army.. 142, 149, 174
Churches Together.. 150
London City Mission 149, 175
Open the Book.. 91, 175
RE Inspired.. 30, 91, 92, 175
Scripture Union 142, 150, 151, 175
Spinnaker Trust.. 149, 175
Church
Activities in school.. 110–113
Community cohesion... 91, 150, 171
Council 32, 36, 40, 98, 112, 115, 116, 123, 125, 126
CRB (see Health and safety)
Helping local 73
Legal responsibility 40, 115, 116
Church building
Benefits of visiting.. 96–97
Candles 103, 107
Churchyard 104, 126
Furnishings.. 100
Information pack 98–99, 104–105
Liturgical colours 102
Planning visits.. 105–106
Risk assessment (see Health and safety)
School services in 157–159
School visits... 96–109
Shape of 99

Signs and symbols 81, 96, 101
Windows.. 99, 101
Collective worship
  Best practice in 55–61
  Bible in.. 58
  Broadly Christian 25, 30, 46, 53
  Challenges in.. 65
  Chaplains leading 55, 140–141
  Inspection of 46, 55
  Leading 55–61
  Led by children.. 54
  Music in (see Music)
  'Pause for thought'.. 55
  Planning... 55, 63–64
  Policy on... 30, 53
  Prayers in... 60–61
  Programmes.. 57–58
  Recording of 55
  Responsibility for 55
  Storytelling in 58–59
Curriculum
  Citizenship 87, 90, 91, 94, 97
  Community cohesion... 91, 150, 171
  Key Stages.. 45
  National 22, 44–45, 89, 128
  PSHE... 58, 87, 89–90, 94
  QCA... 45, 86
  RE (see Religious Education)
  SACRE... 46, 89
  SATs 46, 85, 139
  SEAL 58, 170
Department for Children, Schools and Families.................... 134
Director of Education 137, 173

Drama
    Based on Bible reading 156, 178
    Clubs 111, 118, 126
    Helping with 126
    Performance in church 155–156
Early Years Foundation Stage 45
Education Sunday 28, 36, 157–158
Eucharist
    Children's involvement 76
    Creative arts (use of) 80
    Educational aspect 80–81
    Eucharistic Prayer 179
    Festivals (see Seasons)
    Frequency 78–79
    In school 75–85
    Inclusivity 82
    Living in daily life 81–82
    Manner 79
    Peace, sharing the 82
    Schools' festival (see Cathedrals)
    Signs and symbols (see Church building)
    Step-by-step through the 176–180
Government initiatives (see also Health and safety, Legislation)
    Every Child Matters 38, 42–43, 115, 121
    Extended schools 119, 121–122
    Learning Outside the Classroom 47
    SEAL 58, 170
    Sure Start 145
    Thinking Primary 44
Governors
    Becoming a 137–138
    Composition of 133
    Criteria 48, 130
    Duties of 132, 134–135

Finance 131, 134
Foundation 133
Governance of schools 130
Governing bodies.. 32, 54, 130–132
Local community reps.. 131, 133
Membership 133
Parent.. 133, 137
Pastoral care.. 136–137
Relationship with head teacher................................ 135–136
Health and safety
  Child protection policy 40, 42, 106
  Criminal Records Bureau (CRB) 40–42
  Every Child Matters (see Government initiatives)
  Independent Safeguarding Authority (ISA)...................... 41–42
  Insurance.. 65, 151
  Risk assessment 106
  Safe from Harm.. 186
  Security 33, 41
  Visiting a school.. 43–44
Legislation (see also Government initiatives, Health and safety)
  Butler Education Act 1944.. 21, 51, 86
  Children Act 1989.. 22, 40
  Children Act 2004.. 42
  Education Reform Act 1988 .... 52–53, 86–87
  LEA (see Local authority)
  National Curriculum (see Curriculum)
  Ofsted 25, 32, 39, 44–45, 55, 91, 135
  QCA (see Curriculum)
  SACRE (see Curriculum)
Liturgical colours (see Church building)
Local authority
  Advice and training.. 137
Messy Church 28, 118, 168

Ministry
    Through presence 14–15
    Through service 14
Mission 24–29, 152
Music
    Church services 103
    Concerts 156–157
    Hymns and songs 59
    In collective worship 56, 59, 80
    Instrumental 80
National Society 18–19, 70
Other faiths 60, 83, 132
Parents
    Group 126
    Governors 133, 137
    Helpers 47
    In school 54, 168
    Support for 141
Prayer (see also Worship)
    Areas in school 69
    Candles (see Church building)
    For school 29, 35, 68, 125, 126
    Groups 68, 71–72, 140
    In church 72–73
    In classroom 68–69
    Lord's Prayer 179
    Network 71–72
    Quiet space 71
    School as place of 67–74
    Special situations for 70
Religious Education
    Agreed syllabus 49, 88–89, 92–93
    Barnabas RE Days 37, 170–172

Citizenship (see Curriculum)

Cross-curricular RE 94–95

Helping with 31, 37, 91–94, 124, 148

PSHE (see Curriculum)

RE curriculum 46, 89

RE today 88–89

Reasons for teaching 87–88

The Fourth R (1970) 21–22

Sacraments and other rites

Baptism 81, 100

Eucharist (see Eucharist)

Marriage 81

Reconciliation 81

Schools

Aided 32, 46, 49, 89, 92, 133

Chaplains (see Chaplaincy)

Christian clubs in 117–118

Christian community in 67, 153

Church schools 15, 22, 30, 54, 58, 60, 76, 89, 133, 173

Church service (taking part) 157

Community 30, 46, 133

Controlled 32, 46, 89, 133

Festivals 75

Forming a relationship with 30–37

Foundation 183

Governing bodies (see Governors)

Grant-maintained 22

Methodist 32

Mission 24–26, 32, 152

Ofsted (see Legislation)

Part of parish 26, 96

RE lessons (see Religious Education)

Roman Catholic 32, 75, 173

Teachers (see Teachers)

Visits to church...96–109, 181
Voluntary...19, 20
Voluntary work..124–129
Working in (see Vocation)
Schools' workers (see Chaplaincy, Children's workers)
Seasons
    Advent..102, 171
    Christmas.................35, 73, 94, 95, 100, 102, 154, 159, 171
    Easter..94, 100, 102, 154, 171
    Harvest..73, 95, 128, 154, 159, 171
    Lent..102, 154, 171
    Mothering Sunday 73, 159, 168
    Pentecost...80, 102
Spiritual development....................................25, 51, 75, 86, 88
Storytelling...58–59, 170–171
Sunday school 18, 20
Teachers
    Class 14, 44, 64
    Head 33–34, 54, 93, 116, 128, 133, 135, 166
    Supporting...35, 126, 139, 141
    Visiting churches 97, 105–106
    Vocation of (see Vocation)
Uniformed organisations (see Children's activities)
Using school building
    Advantages of 119–120, 162
    Respect for..164–165
    School equipment..165
Visitors 63–64
Visual aids 57
Vocation
    In daily life..11–14
    Teaching 14–16
    Working in school..14–15

Voluntary help

    Accountability 20, 98, 115–116

    Appropriate behaviour 128–129

    Church council 126

    Clergy and lay leaders 127

    Criteria for volunteers 124–125

    Helping in class 126–127

    Identifying 124–125

    Support for 33

Worship (see also Church, Collective worship, Eucharist, Prayer, Sacraments)

    Church worshipping in school 162–168

    Common Worship 77–78, 179

    In Christian schools 54

    In school since 1944 51–54

    Presence of God 53, 57, 61, 79, 96, 108, 117, 166–167

    Sacred space 96, 166–168

    Worship area 69

More Collective Worship Unwrapped

20 tried and tested story-based assemblies for primary schools

John Guest

More Collective Worship Unwrapped is a flexible and practical resource, ideal for all who are seeking to grasp the key principles of collective worship as quickly and as effectively as possible. The material is equally valuable for both newly qualified and experienced teachers, as well as RE coordinators and those invited into schools to lead collective worship.

Following the success of *Collective Worship Unwrapped*, this second book provides a further 20 story-based assemblies to use with Key Stages 1 and 2. As before, each of the assemblies gives a Bible base, tips on presentation, visual aids required, recommended songs, an optional prayer and follow-up material.

Once again, the stories have all been written for live situations. Their inspiration has come from many sources but, above all, each one is based on and inspired by stories from the Bible. Each outline can be set in the context of a variety of topical themes, including moral and personal development, citizenship, spiritual values, seasons of the Christian year and special times.

ISBN 978 1 84101 664 1   £12.99
Available from your local Christian bookshop or, in case of difficulty, direct from BRF using the order form opposite.

Resourcing **Collective Worship and Assemblies, RE, Festivals, Drama** and **Art** in primary schools

- Barnabas RE Days—exploring Christianity creatively
- INSET
- Books and resources
- www.barnabasinschools.org.uk

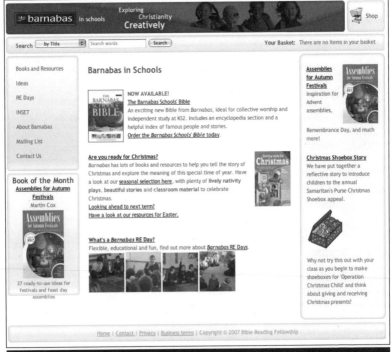